ENDOR**S**

"Louise has written a book of incredible encouragement. She weaves life experiences together with Scripture and provides penetrating insights on how to cope with the many physical and emotional challenges of aging."

> —DR. DAVE REAGAN, FOUNDER OF LAMB AND LION MINISTRIES, WITH A WEEKLY INTERNATIONAL TELEVISION PROGRAM

"Louise Looney offers insights, told with her great sense of humor and down-to-earth wisdom. *Make the Rest of Your Days the Best of Your Days* makes the reader want to pick up their spiritual metal detector and look for the golden rewards in the aging process."

> —TRAVIS WINN, RETIRED SUPERINTENDENT OF PUBLIC SCHOOLS

"Make the Rest of Your Days the Best of Your Days addresses the challenges of aging with honesty and humor. Encouragement and practical help to live your life to the fullest and be a blessing to others. You'll be inspired to joyfully embrace each day and to find gold while growing old. Highly recommended."

> —MARLENE BAGNULL, LITT.D. AUTHOR, SPEAKER, EDITOR, PUBLISHER, DIRECTOR OF THE COLORADO AND GREATER PHILADELPHIA CHRISTIAN WRITER'S CONFERENCES (WWW.WRITEHISANSWER.COM)

"Louise's gentle and witty personality floods the pages of her new book *Make the Rest of Your Days, the Best of Your Days*. It's a delightful book that kept me smiling through every skillfully written chapter."

> —ROY HANSCHKE, MORNING SHOW HOST, AM91.ORG

"To keep the spring in your step when winter is on your head, you'll want to read Louise Looney's book *Make the Rest of Your Days, the Best of Your Days*. With her unique wit and wisdom you'll find new perspective on aging that offers hope and fruitfulness in every season of life."

—ALAN SPLAWN, ASSOCIATE PASTOR OF A MEGA CHURCH

"It is encouraging to know how God can use us in our 'sunset years.' Each chapter has tidbits that can be applied to any age. Thank you, Louise, for the laughter and insight."

—LYNN NEWALD, SENIOR VICE-PRESIDENT AT NATION STAR
MORTGAGE WITH 8,000 EMPLOYEES

"A must read for seniors! Louise Looney, has created a masterpiece in *Make the Rest of Your Days the Best of Your Days.* In this wonderful book, she presents readers with a biblical perspective on aging."

—JANICE THOMPSON, AWARD-WINNING AUTHOR

"Louise Looney is the youngest "old" person I know. Her eternal joy and love of life makes many "young" people seem years older than she. I highly recommend this warm, witty, and wise young author!"

—JAMES N. WATKINS, AWARD-WINNING AUTHOR AND SPEAKER

"As an author, Louise Looney's writings overflow with wisdom gleaned by experience. Our ministry has substantially grown using her writings. Her encouragement empowers people to be a blessing regardless of age."

—TOM AND SUE HOBDY (AVID FANS)

Make the

of Your Days
the

Best

of Your Days

Louise L. Looney

Make the Rest of Your Days, The Best of Your Days
First published as *Hidden Treasures for Golden Years*, XP Publishing, 2011
Copyright © 2011, 2017 Louise L. Looney

ISBN-13: 978-1981163038

Printed in the United States of America

Cover Designer: James Mathew
Typesetter (publisher)
Editor: Marlene Bagnull

TABLE OF CONTENTS

ACKNOWLEDGEMENTS

Thanks to my cheering section who urged me to write this message. I'm grateful to Sam Lanford who read the manuscript and gave me great suggestions and feedback. Gratitude is also due to Joanne Hillman who critiqued the book and gave helpful input. Bette Lanahan came numerous times to help me wrestle with a rebellious computer, viruses, and a cranky printer. With her prayers she spurred me on. Marlene Bagnull picked me up when I became discouraged and took time from her jam-packed schedule to read and offer encouraging comments. Countless others kept me on track.

Most of all, I'm grateful to my Heavenly Father who gently nudged me and sometimes pushed me to complete the work He assigned me. He taught me to depend on Him through prayer and gave me insightful and encouraging words to pass on to His older children. I concluded—if He chose me, He can certainly choose you!

INTRODUCTION

*M*ake the Rest of Your Days the Best of Your Days is a revision of *Hidden Treasures for Golden Years*. It contains additional stories and has a more powerful message of hope and encouragement for the maturing Christian.

Hopefully, the reader will discover a plan and purpose for his own life. Ecclesiastes 12, Solomon gives a rather dismal description of what happens to an aging body. However, God challenges us to focus on the beauty of the inner man and discover what He wants to accomplish there.

It is my prayer the reader's faith will grow strong as he gains insight into the marvelous plan our Heavenly Father has for this season of life. May they discover the hidden treasures in His Word that deal with attitudes and the condition of the heart, rather than striving to look good on the outside.

Instead of a tiny sparkle, like a firefly flipping off and on, I pray the reader will be a light that grows brighter and brighter as they draw closer to the Son.

The purpose of this book is to inspire believers to cultivate a godly life that radiates from within. This new creation changes us from the inside out.

NOTE

Some names have been changed to protect their identity.

ECCLESIASTES 12:1–8, 13

Remember your Creator in the days of your youth,
before the days of trouble come
and the years approach when you will say,
"I find no pleasure in them"—
before the sun and the light
and the moon and the stars grow dark,
and the clouds return after the rain;
when the keepers of the house tremble,
and the strong men stoop,
when the grinders cease because they are few,
and those looking through the windows grow dim;
when the doors to the street are closed
and the sound of grinding fades;
when people rise up at the sound of birds,
but all their songs grow faint;
when people are afraid of heights
and of dangers in the streets;
when the almond tree blossoms
and the grasshopper drags himself along
and desire no longer is stirred.
Then people go to their eternal home
and mourners go about the streets.
Remember him—before the silver cord is severed,
and the golden bowl is broken;
before the pitcher is shattered at the spring,
and the wheel broken at the well,
and the dust returns to the ground it came from,
and the spirit returns to God who gave it.
"Meaningless! Meaningless!" says the Teacher.
"Everything is meaningless!"
Now all has been heard;
here is the conclusion of the matter:
Fear God and keep his commandments,
for this is the duty of all mankind.

1

WHERE DID THEY HIDE THE GOLD?

I am certain that God, who began the good work within you, will continue his work until it is finally finished on the day when Christ Jesus returns.
Philippians 1:6 NLT

I scratched my head and wondered. *Why do they call these the golden years?* Though I have gold in my teeth, no one seems interested in the silver in my hair or the gas on my stomach. *Tell me one more time how valuable life is when these body parts begin to wear out.* Perhaps I should borrow a metal detector and go hunting for the gold, supposedly hidden somewhere between here and eternity.

The world declares I've reached the time when I'm "over the hill." That should imply I should be able to coast for the rest of the way, right? *Wrong.* I listen carefully, but I can't hear God tell me it's okay to lean back, take it easy, and watch the world go by.

Some Think We're of Value

Perhaps we should ask the opinion of those who think we're of great value. Grandchildren usually think we're special. My sister's granddaughter climbed up in her lap and began to stroke her cheeks. "Meme, I love your skin. I *love* your skin." My sister smiled as she relished this this lovely compliment. "Thank you, honey, you're so sweet."

Her granddaughter slid off her lap, scrunched her shoulders, and giggled. "It's sooo loose."

My sister's countenance fell as her self-image slipped down the tube. Afterwards, I went in the bathroom and stared in the mirror. My loose skin was a shocker, with a wattle of flesh drooping beneath my chin. My face had trails of wrinkles connecting every nook and cranny. And when I stepped out of the shower the next morning, I was not pleased with the reflection I saw in the mirror. Most of my body parts had moved south. Fully clothed and well camouflaged, I look bad enough. Stark naked, I'm a pitiful sight. So, I think I'll be like those mentioned in James 1:23–24 who see themselves in a mirror, walk away, and forget what they look like.

How Others Look at Aging

The impact of what others think about aging came when I roomed with a gorgeous young model at a seminar. She spent hours in the bathroom every morning attempting to look flawless and beautiful. It disturbed me—especially when I needed to get in the bathroom for a few minutes. I confronted her. "What will you do when you can no longer cover up every blemish and fine-line wrinkle?"

She looked astonished. "I can't imagine living past the age of thirty."

My heart sank. But then again, when I find new wrinkles etched across my face, you won't hear me shouting hallelujah. And I'm not too happy about other signs of aging. Perhaps it is time to search the Scriptures to see what God intends for these blustery winter seasons of life when our bodies begin to show our age.

I decided to check with the wisest man who ever lived to see if he had answers. This led me to Ecclesiastes 12 where Solomon explains a number of things that happen when age begins to take its toll. Great! The chapter is filled with one phrase after another, listing things that go wrong during these ongoing years. Thank you very much,

Solomon. I can't tell you how much I needed to be reminded of all the things that fall apart during the aging process.

I felt a gentle tap on my shoulder and a whisper caught my attention. "The things Solomon spoke of are cold facts, but he spoke of the physical body. Dig deeper and you'll find the exciting plans I have for a vibrant new life I designed for the inside where real beauty counts." This made me realize that regardless of what happens to this earth-suit, God wants us to joyfully anticipate things He's working on that will keep our hearts forever young.

My heart beat faster. A tingle went up my spine as I realized the depth and breadth of the Scripture. "People judge by outward appearance, but the LORD looks at the heart" (1 Sam. 16:7 NLT). It was time for me to look at life from God's perspective.

The mystery regarding these invisible treasures for later years began to unfold. Tiny glimpses motivated me to study God's Word to discover what He would show me as I walked through these evening shadows of life.

Come—go with me on this exciting journey. We'll scan the pages of other people's lives to find those who have successfully navigated these rough waters. Perhaps we can discover how God orchestrates circumstances to create something of incredible beauty and value.

As I recalled events from the past, I began to get a glimpse of God's magnificent plan. Lessons came from the young and the old, the simple and the brilliant. They challenged me to make a paradigm shift, from the focus on the outside body to the inside, where God's transformation is to take place. One particular Scripture spurred me on. "And I am certain that God, who began the good work within you, will continue his work until it is finally finished on the day when Christ Jesus returns" (Phil. 1:6 NLT).

The Lord encouraged me to take each phrase of Ecclesiastes 12 and dissect it to see what was concealed beneath the surface—at the core—where seeds could be watered to grow into a beautiful *inner* man. Each small discovery revealed our Father's wisdom in this new creation that will live with Him forever in His kingdom.

3

LIFE APPLICATION

1. Have you wondered why we have to go through the aging process?
2. What virtues do you think God wants to develop as we age?
3. Do you believe God has a purpose in everything that happens as we grow older?
4. Are there aspects of aging that discourage you?
5. Are you willing to search for meaning in this season of life?
6. Do you know someone who has remained upbeat and cheerful as they aged?
7. How much does attitude have to do with contentment?
8. What do you think it means when Scripture says God looks at your heart?
9. Are you more concerned with what others think, or what God thinks?
10. How much time and money do you spend trying to look younger?

2
WHERE DID MY MEMORY GO?

Remember your Creator in the days of your youth.
Ecclesiastes 12:1

Solomon begins this passage with the discouraging announcement that we're to remember God when we're young. If this is necessary, some of us missed it. There are many things about the past most of us would like to redo, but our youth is long gone. If we failed to honor God when we were young, is there hope for us at this late date?

Our Savior Jesus is called the Redeemer. As a Redeemer, I'm sure He's perfectly capable of setting us free from the past, regardless of what we've done or failed to do. We still have the privilege of developing a deep and meaningful relationship with our Heavenly Father. If we are willing to draw near to Him, He will draw near to us. He lifts us from our doldrums and surrounds us with love and compassion. The time we spend getting to know God better now can overshadow any deficit we had in younger years.

No physical exertion is needed to create a bond with our Heavenly Father. In earlier years, I thought I had to work my head off to stay on God's good side. I pictured myself hanging over a fiery caldron by a thread which the Righteous Judge threatened to snip if I made one false move. As I studied the Word, however, I discovered it's not about my efforts. It's all about His amazing grace.

5

God Always Had His Eye on Us

It thrilled me to learn God has had His eye on us all along, even before we were born. "You made all the delicate, inner parts of my body and knit me together in my mother's womb" (Ps.139:13 NLT). He was there when we didn't have a clue He was anywhere around. In eternity, we'll likely stand in awe when our past is unveiled. We'll discover countless times when God protected us from danger and/or disaster.

While we may not have been fully aware of our Creator in our younger years, it's obvious He has always been aware of us. For instance, my parents told me I fell into a pond and almost drowned when I was a three-year-old. When they frantically rescued me, I was unconscious. God mercifully performed a miracle to revive me. It's quite clear He watched over me then.

When I was ten years old, a conniving stranger urged me to go with him. I followed a short distance before a feeling of caution swept over me and I turned back while still in view of adults who stood nearby. I'm confident the Lord protected me. I praise God for the times He kept me safe.

Childlike Ways

We played a game once in which a player had to read and answer a question. My husband drew a card that asked for an appropriate epitaph for his spouse's tombstone. "I think I'd put, 'She's the oldest little girl I know.'" Hopefully, he referred to childlike characteristics of joy, forgiveness, and trust. I'd like that. I want to be childlike, but not childish.

Don't Focus on Past Regrets

We may think of the past with nostalgia rather than remembering how God kept watch over us in bygone days. We drag mementos from the closet in the form of photo albums, yellowed newspaper clippings, ribbons, and trophies in order to hang on to snippets of bygone days. Careful! As we sort through these memories, we mustn't be disheartened and see them as evidence we've now passed into a "has-been" status.

It's highly unlikely our children will want to keep these trophies, and the Lord knows they won't sell in a garage sale. After we're gone, our accomplishments may be shoved to the back shelf of people's minds. The mementos themselves may be tossed out to be hauled away with the trash.

Satan no doubt is standing nearby, watching for ways to trip us up in our reminiscing. He weasels in to spin his devious web by binding up our joy and immobilizing our hope for the days ahead. He permeates our thought-life with memories of the way things "used to be" or "should have been" in an attempt to trap us in a web of yesteryears.

To foil the devil's schemes, we need to leave intangible but beautiful memories—mental trophies of encouragement. What a delight to realize it's never too late to prepare a treasure chest of love and tender concern for our heirs. We can choose to leave a storehouse of delightful memories. Go ahead. Let the executors of our wills discard our awards and ribbons. We'll have a much better legacy for those whose lives we've touched.

Dealing with Bad Memories

Years ago at midnight, my niece was attacked, kidnapped, and dragged into a vacant house where her assailant slit her throat, raped her, and left her to die. She survived by pretending to be dead, so he would stop stabbing her. Miraculously, after her attacker left, she crawled to a nearby house where the people who were still up called an ambulance to rush her to the hospital. Against all odds, she survived. Doctors told her parents, "There are five reasons she shouldn't have lived." Police warned her parents, "She'll likely need counseling for the rest of her life."

God mercifully had a thoracic surgeon on duty the night of her tragedy. He told her family, "When her assailant cut her throat, he missed the jugular vein by a fraction of an inch." Days later, when she stabilized, this doctor challenged her. "You have a choice as to how you handle this horrific assault. You can get counseling and work through it—or you can stuff it, and it will haunt you for the rest of your life." Thankfully, she chose to take his advice and found emotional healing.

As God would have it, He took that atrocity and wrapped it in a soft blanket of His mercy, and she overcame the horrors of that ordeal. Our Lord watered her seed-like faith to help her develop an attitude of dogged determination and to defeat the schemes of the evil one who was bent on her destruction. She resolutely declared, "That man ruined a portion of my life, but by God's grace, he will not ruin the rest of it." She'll never forget the attack, but because God enfolded her with His loving care, the terrorizing experience was unable to paralyze her.

Wonder of wonders, she now works in an inner city ministry that reaches out to former prisoners, indigents, and homeless men who have been involved in all sorts of crimes. Some of them may have been guilty of wicked and cruel assaults similar to the one she experienced. But she is dedicated in working with these men, so they can redeem their past and become worthwhile citizens who give—rather than take—from society.

Though we can't change our past, God can heal damaging blows from bad encounters. He encourages us to gradually open our clenched fists and to release our hurts and fears for His healing touch. He tenderly massages each troubled spot until it loses its power to hold us in its clutch.

Our Lord helps us work through bad memories until they can actually become a factor in our growing stronger. He blesses us with a gift of faith to trust Him with our pain. "The person who lives in right relationship with God does it by embracing what God arranges for him" (Gal. 3:11 MSG). We hold steady while He spreads a healing balm on wounds of the past.

Forgiveness Is to Remove Guilt

Satan's evil assaults show up in many different ways. He stirs up fear, anger, and self-pity to muddle our thinking until it is difficult to see God. The enemy attempts to use our past mistakes to rob us of our peace, steal our joy, and destroy our future. But when he reminds us of our past, it's time for us to remind him of his future!

The apostle Paul had a sordid track record of murdering and persecuting Christians, yet he announced, "One thing I do, forgetting the things which are behind, and stretching forward to the things which are before, I press on toward the goal unto the prize of the high calling of God in Christ Jesus" (Phil. 3:13–14 ASV). Paul knew if he kept dwelling on his past sins, he would be of no value in his new life in Christ. He trusted God to deal with the after-effects of the murder of Christians and the trail of widows and orphans he left behind. Paul's repentance caused God to treat his sins like water under the bridge. He washed them out to sea, never to be remembered again. It's time for us to lift our bad experiences to God and pray, "Gracious Father, toss them overboard."

For years, I struggled with guilt because I stole a nickel as a child and cheated on some exams in college. Satan claimed squatter's rights in my mind with his accusations. But I found I could refuse to listen to instant replays of everything I'd done wrong. If I continued to kick myself, it would be like a slap in God's face—implying Jesus' crucifixion wasn't enough to pay for my sins.

Every time Satan drags a bag of bad memories back into our minds, we can refuse to listen to his accusations by telling him: "When you try to place a heavy weight of guilt on me, I'll use it as a reminder to praise God, because He provided a way for me to be forgiven. Since our Father inhabits the praises of His people, this should send the tormentor scrambling!

Jehovah Knows Our Needs

When the economy went belly-up in the fall of 2008, I was shaken.

The stock market crashed and I lost about a third of everything I had. We'd already lost our retirement money in a bad investment, and I'd quit working (for a salary) years before. My initial provider, my husband, was gone. As I grumbled and stewed over my losses, God whispered in my spirit, *Have I not taken good care of you?*

I thought back. When my husband died, my friend, a financial adviser told me, "You have enough money to last approximately five years. If you aren't careful, you'll be broke then." It has been thirty years since my husband's death. Time and again, God has been Jehovah Jireh, my Provider. "Thank You, Lord. You *have* taken care of me in extraordinary ways." My Heavenly Father continues to be with me, even when money runs out before the end of the month.

I was blessed with the opportunity to manage a Christian Retreat Center called Hidden Manna, and God provided me with other income. People have financed mission trips, and all my needs have been supplied.

Remember the Good

Shortly after my husband died, I went to Israel during the Feast of Tabernacles. This is a week of celebration with the Jewish tradition of eating outdoors under a shelter. This is in remembrance of the forty years the Israelites lived in tents when Moses led them through the wilderness to the land of Canaan.

While I was there, a former US ambassador invited us to his home for dinner. The meal was served outside, under a canopy. Our host explained a wonderful tradition: "Family members aren't to complain about anything this week. At mealtime, our conversations are to be centered on the goodness of God and what He's done in each of our lives." How delightful it would be to sit around the table and share memories of our loving Father. The gratitude expressed in this experience would tend to crowd out all the negative cares of the world.

Be Patient—It's Not Too Late

Since our lives are a mixed bag of hurry-up-and-wait, we tend to struggle with impatience. God encourages us to wait for His timing. The Holy Spirit can teach us the virtue of holding steady in the midst of a world that seems to be spinning out of control. He helps us to be sensitive to know when to move forward and when to stand still.

How comforting to wake up every morning knowing God is the same as He's always been. He never changes. "Because of the LORD'S great love, we are not consumed, for his compassions never fail. They are new every morning; great is your faithfulness" (Lam. 3:22–24).

If you failed to remember the Lord in the days of your youth, it's not too late. Read the parable of the men sent to work in the vineyard in Matthew 20:1–16. The men who came to work near the end of the day were paid a full day's wage. We find Jehovah is often the God of the eleventh hour. One of the men who died on the cross next to Jesus asked for and received forgiveness only hours before his death.

One of my relatives had been alienated from her mother for years. When her mom was critically ill, she visited her in hospice care. Each asked the other for forgiveness and prayed and wept with joy with one another. As her mother's life faded, her daughter spent countless hours at her bedside. She read her Scriptures, sang her mother's favorite songs, massaged her arms and legs with lotion, and spoke lovingly to her. The nurse commented, "How peacefully your mother lies there during her final days." Her daughter became what God asked her to be—a minister of reconciliation.

I'm thankful we're not too old to crawl into the lap of our Abba Father—to thank and praise Him for being loving and trustworthy from the days of our youth. We can confidently hold on to our Heavenly Father while reaching out to lift others to Him.

Life Application

1. Share a time when it was evident God was with you.
2. Is there some trauma or hurt from the past that still troubles you?
3. Why is it bad to dwell on bad things from the past?
4. What do you want people to remember about you after you're gone?
5. Do you remember to thank God for the things He's done for you?
6. Is there anyone with whom you need to be reconciled?
7. Do you continue to kick yourself for the bad things you've done?
8. What good memories will you leave with others?
9. In talking to others, are you more negative or positive?
10. Are you committed to grow closer to God?

3
TROUBLE COMES TROMPING IN

... before the days of trouble come ...
Ecclesiastes 12:1

Have you ever wondered what it would be like to live in a trouble-free world? Adam and Eve were the only ones who've been blessed with this experience. But things changed drastically when they sinned. Mankind got off on the wrong foot soon after they stepped on planet earth.

We know now it is not a matter of, *if* trouble comes, but rather, *when.* "I have told you these things, so that in me you may have peace. In this world you will have trouble. But take heart! I have overcome the world" (John 16:33).

Family Troubles

When I arrived on the scene, my birth spelled trouble. Mom became pregnant with me, the eighth child, in the depths of the Great Depression. Neither she nor Dad turned cartwheels the day they realized I was on the way. My debut would offer no reason for celebration. However, when I was born, Mom gathered me under her wing, like a mother hen, with all the rest of her chicks.

Trouble dogged my dad's heels almost everywhere he went.

When I was only a few weeks old, he had a terrible accident. As he unhitched the team used to pull a plow, one of the mules kicked him in his forehead and crushed the front of his skull. My brother, Don, saw him crawling toward the house with blood streaming down his face. He and two of my other brothers rushed to him and helped him into the car. They and our mother drove at high speeds to the hospital where the doctor told them. "He'll not make it through the night."

During the long hours when the medical team fought to save my father's life, our sleep-deprived Mom drummed her fingers in nervous silence. My older brother, Rex, gripped the arms of his chair and cautiously asked, "What are we going to do?" Mom pursed her lips like a tightened drawstring. "We pray." She not only prayed for his life, but she also thanked God as Dad began to recover. Time after time, when subsequent accidents occurred, she chose this same approach.

Trouble assaulted Dad on other occasions with the loss of a finger and other fingers mangled when a crooked stick threw his hand into the whirling blade of a circular saw. He lost an eye when an anhydrous ammonia coupling came loose and blew up in his face. He had broken bones and other injuries until he became so crippled he had to use two canes to walk.

Handicaps failed to squelch his determination. He would not succumb to defeat. When a calamity broadsided him, he prayed. Even now, I smile as I remember when I heard his knees crack in church; I knew he was kneeling to pray.

One year, our normally drought-ridden farm was almost washed away with a flood. "Oh no," my brother cried. "The water is rising in the bottom fields ruining our crops. Is this ever gonna stop?"

"Son, never forget who sends the rain," Dad chided. "The Lord sends the rain on the just and the unjust."

My father fought with dogged determination to keep trouble from getting the upper hand. All our lives, our large vegetable garden furnished food for our family and neighbors. After all we children grew up and left home, Dad continued gardening.

We cringed when we learned he was hobbling out to the garden, sliding his hands down his canes until he fell to his knees and crawled up and down the rows—cultivating, planting, weeding, and harvesting. He wouldn't let age and crippling arthritis cause him to throw up his hands and quit.

Under the worst of circumstances, when others asked Dad how he was doing, he'd smile and nod in affirmation. "Thank you, I'm tolerable." Shortly before he died, he told us, "I only wish I'd known that during the hardest of times, I didn't have to do it alone." The lesson he learned late in life became a legacy he passed on to his children. He taught us when trouble is too high to climb over and too wide to go around, Jesus will always help us face the trouble head-on.

At Dad's funeral, the minister said he'd watched him many times in church—standing, leaning on his canes, and singing in harmony with his booming bass voice. "He reminded me of the Scripture describing the patriarch Jacob as he leaned over his staff and worshipped God." He added, "But now, your father enjoys the glorious new body God has prepared for him."

Achor—the Valley of Trouble

Murphy's Law says, "Anything that can possibly go wrong, will go wrong." However, this is neither biblical nor God's plan.

The Valley of Achor, referred to in Joshua 7:26, means the Valley of Trouble. My dad was not the only one who frequently found himself in that valley. Many of you have been there. But the Lord never intended for any of us to list Achor as our permanent address.

Discouragement loses its case when God added in Scripture, "There I will … transform her Valley of Trouble into a Door of Hope" (Hos. 2:15 TLB). This shouts loud and clear that God will provide a doorway of hope every time we find ourselves trapped in a Valley of Trouble.

Doorways of hope are difficult to see when we're preoccupied—looking down and mulling over bad circumstances. This is the time to ask the Lord for the courage to look up and find that door of hope. It will surely open if we persist in asking, knocking, and seeking.

Clinging to a thread of hope is a challenge, especially when we can't see any solution to our dilemma. Christ encourages us to hold steady. Hope gives us the courage to lift our heads and strength for our frail bodies to keep moving forward.

Trouble tends to distract us from following through with God's plans. Hard times are often wrapped in a package of confusion and frustration and tied with a ribbon of self-pity. It arrives on our doorstep marked, *Special Delivery.*

Some see no way to adapt or adjust to stay on top of a situation:

> Too many mope,
> Trying to cope,
> Failing to look,
> For the doorway of hope.

There's no need to be caught off-guard. When trouble knocks at the door, we'll ask Jesus to go with us to face and overcome our problems. Somewhat like a door-to-door salesman, who comes to sell his wares, the enemy regularly tries to peddle a load of worrisome situations. We can resist his attempt to force his way in. We must stomp our foot and refuse to buy his lies.

Worrying about Tomorrow

If we take yesterday's problems, add today's struggles, and pile on the potential of things that could go wrong tomorrow, our emotions may well register *tilt.* The muscles of our character are strengthened when we exercise our God-given ability to conquer one problem at a time. "So don't worry about tomorrow, because tomorrow will have its own worries. Each day has enough troubles of its own" (Matt. 6:34 NCV).

View Problems from God's Perspective

I met a beautiful woman who was born to an unwed mother but adopted soon after her birth. That family loved her and gave her every advantage a biological child could want or need. They gave her voice lessons to develop the exceptional talent she later used for her livelihood and to sing praises to the Lord. In spite of this seemingly blessed life, she still felt rejected and abandoned.

In a private conversation I said, "Danielle, your birth parents may not have planned you, but God did. He fashioned the exact DNA from your birth parents for the unique purpose He had in mind for your life. I'd like to think the moment you were conceived, the angels shouted across heaven, 'Danielle is on her way!'"

This lady began to look at her life from a different perspective. She realized she probably wouldn't have been so blessed if she'd remained with her birth mother. What once she viewed as a problem, she now saw as an open door of opportunity to fulfill the glorious plan God had in mind for her.

Commit to Give Everything to God

It's difficult to let go of our troubles, but we have scriptures we can trust: "I know whom I have believed, and am convinced that he is able to guard that which I have committed unto him against that day" (2 Tim. 1:12). We may offer bits and pieces of our lives to God, picking and choosing what we're willing to give to Him. But we need to remind ourselves, "If He only guards the things we've committed to Him, why would we cling to one iota of any bad situation?"

In Bible class one Sunday, a lady committed to give everything she had to the Lord. The next week, as she drove home from church, her car caught fire. She jumped out and stood nearby to watch it burn and asked, "Lord, why are you burning *Your* car?" An amazing peace swept over her heart when she reasoned, "Since I gave everything to Him, I suppose He can do whatever He wants with it." Soon after, she experienced an unexpected blessing when a friend offered to give her another car, better than the one destroyed.

Give It to God

You've likely heard the expression, "If you give a man enough rope, he may well hang himself." I've gotten so tangled up trying to deal with circumstances that both the rope and I became frazzled. Someone advised, "When you get to the end of your rope, you should tie a knot and hang on." However, it would far better if we handed the rope to God for Him to pull us out of our messes. He is our lifeline.

When I focus on my problems, I become distressed.
When I realize my inadequacies, I feel depressed.
When I give it all to God, I'm totally blessed.

Each time we pass a test in life, we may sigh with relief and say with the little train engine, "I thought I could! I thought I could!" With our spiritual eyes, we might also envision Jesus in the background whispering, "I knew you could! I knew you could!"

No Excuses for Being Rude

My husband, Carey, walked in the door, his distraught expression a reflection of his mood. "You'll not believe what just happened. I went to close the deal on the sale of our farm, and the potential buyer didn't even show up. That means we have no money to pay the huge balloon note due on our town house next week."

He'd hardly gotten the words out of his mouth when the phone rang. "Yes, I understand, Mrs. Jones," he said. "The note is due on Monday. But please let me tell you what just happened. We may need a few extra days." After he explained our plight, he jerked the phone away from his ear. The woman who had owner-financed our home shouted curses and threatened charges.

Carey listened to her tirade for several minutes before he interrupted. "Mrs. Jones, we've never missed a payment. Until Monday, the note is our problem. We may need a little extra time, but you can count on it. We'll come up with the money as soon as possible."

Hanging up the phone, he shook his head. "She's been a bear to work with ever since we bought this town home from her."

The next morning, Carey scrambled to borrow money from every resource he could think of, including loans on our two cars. By God's grace, he was able to scrape the money together by the weekend. We went to the title company on Monday with a check in hand. After the deal closed, the legal representatives left the room. Carey raised his hand, "Wait, Mrs. Jones, I have something I need to talk to you about."

"What do you want?"

"Louise and I have been married for thirty-five years. During that period of time, we have bought and sold twenty homes. In all those transactions, we've never dealt with anyone who has been as consistently rude as you have been."

"Wha … well, uh, I'm under a lot of pressure. My husband has been sick."

Carey stood there, gaunt and yellowed with jaundice because of cancer and liver failure. "It *is* difficult to be kind when you're under pressure and in pain, but that's no excuse for being rude."

Mrs. Jones sputtered and walked away.

Carey was dead in six weeks, but he left a beautiful example of holding steady in the midst of a heap of his own troubles.

We Will Have Trials

Trials seem to be a part of the process of becoming a mature Christian. Aging comes with many *opportunities* for us to grow strong as children of our Heavenly Father. We decide whether to accept what's happening to our bodies, as opposed to expressing a nasty, kicking-and-screaming attitude.

We'd never know whether we were totally committed if we were never tested. Our faith is like gold that is refined by fire. When gold is exposed to high temperatures, the dross rises to the top and is skimmed away. In a similar way, trials turn up the heat in our lives, and our impure thoughts and attitudes float to the surface. We can't squirm out of this purifying process. "May God himself, the God of peace, sanctify you through and through" (1 Thess. 5:23). If Shadrach, Meshach, and Abednego came out of a fiery furnace unscathed, we can too.

When we lived in Wyoming and Colorado, I often drove on ice and constantly reminded myself, "Don't hit the brakes. Don't hit the brakes." When life's struggles confront us, we may hear Jesus whisper, "Don't hit the panic button." Our own reasoning and capabilities are inadequate. We need the God of the universe to lead us across the slippery spots in life.

Trust the Outcome to God

The road mapped out for us sometimes feels like an obstacle course. Regardless of the difficulties, we know we'll win if we follow the Lord. Our Father won't take us anywhere we can't emerge better and stronger.

> "No test or temptation that comes your way is beyond the course of what others have had to face. All you need to remember is that God will never let you be pushed past your limit; he'll always be there to help you come through it" (1 Cor. 10:13 MSG).

We Have Problems Understanding

My son, Paul, was asked by a friend to visit a man in prison. "He's asked to see you." Paul remembered Jesus told us we are to visit those who are sick and in prison. He drove to the jail and stood in the heat behind a long line, slowly working his way to the window. When he reached the receptionist, she told him the prisoner was in Building B.

Paul walked to the second building, only to find a longer line than the first. Finally, at the desk, they informed him that the man was in a third unit. Paul breathed a long sigh and went to Building C. The line was not as long, but he was sweaty and tired. When he reached the window, they asked for his identification and he showed them his driver's license. The attendant looked at the records and refused to let him go in. "Your name is not on the visitor's list."

Paul shook his head and walked away. He reasoned, "Lord, I

believe You nudged me to go to the prison. I went out of obedience to You. I'm not responsible for what happened and refuse to get upset." We too must commit to being obedient to God and trust Him, regardless of how a situation turns out.

Though trouble comes early and stays late, we can find comfort and hope in every situation. Our magnificent Father gives us the ability not only to hold steady, but also to grow stronger in an overcoming walk.

LIFE APPLICATION

1. Does anyone you know get upset about every little thing that goes wrong?
2. Do you believe God offers a doorway of hope in each difficult circumstance?
3. Do bad things distract you from the focus you're to have in life?
4. Did God make you the way you are for a special purpose?
5. How can we be sure God will go through our troubles with us?
6. Are you willing to commit everything to God?
7. Can you think of any good that has come from bad situations you've faced?
8. Are your feelings or circumstances an excuse for a rotten attitude?
9. Do you come through struggles stronger or weaker than you were before?
10. Are you confident God will go through your troubles with you?

4

I CAN NO LONGER SAY, "I SEE"

... the sun and the light and the moon and the stars grow dark ...
Ecclesiastes 12:2

In this Scripture, Solomon writes about age bringing about the curse of failing eyesight. This becomes a reality when we can no longer read street signs and a haze seems to cover our surroundings because the lenses of our eyes no longer see sharp images. This frustrating malady is evident in poor night vision, glaucoma, macular degeneration, cataracts, and overall poor vision. Enough said—you get the picture—although you may not be able to see it well.

It's our eyesight fading, rather than the sun and moon and stars growing dark. Lack of clarity won't allow us to say, "I see." God's light fixtures burn as brightly as ever, but poor vision keeps us from seeing them clearly.

Perhaps you've had the same difficulty I experienced in my forties when I began to push a book farther and farther away. I wondered, "Is osteoporosis causing my arms to shrink, along with my height?" The truth smacked me in the face. My eyes were the source of the problem. Then an encouraging Scripture popped up: "Surely the arm of the LORD is not too short" (Isa. 59:1). *Lord, do you mind holding the book for me?*

Others experience the same problems as their eyesight begins to dim.

- From single-vision glasses to bifocals and then trifocals.
- Glasses on, glasses off, squinting to focus.
- Lost glasses. (I feel ridiculous when I find them on top of my head.)
- Trying to ignore the spots floating across my field of vision.
- Needing a magnifying glass to read small print.

I wasn't pleased when my ophthalmologist told me, "I won't be able to totally correct your vision."

"Why?"

"It's your age. Besides that, you have a wrinkled retina."

Oh, my word! My eyeballs are also getting wrinkled! They must be crinkling up as well as my skin. Since my flesh is beginning to look like crepe, perhaps I should change my name to Myrtle, and everyone could just call me the name of the flowering tree, "Crepe Myrtle." There is one consolation as our eyesight becomes worse. Perhaps we won't be so aware of the poor shape of our bodies!

Light Is a Powerful Resource

God placed great emphasis on light. At the dawn of creation, our all-powerful Creator shouted, and light exploded throughout the universe to banish the darkness. He called for light, and it streamed across the heavens and lit up the skies. The sun brightened the day in order for us to find our way around. He provided the night with soft moonlight, surrounded by a starry host, to set the tone for love and rest.

Light enables us to enjoy beautiful sunsets, waterfalls, lakes, flowers, and trees. It seems ironic: Now that we have the time to stop and enjoy their beauty, we can't see as well as we once did. How true the statement: We often don't appreciate a gift until it's gone.

Keep Your Eyes Open

My siblings were fun-loving and welcomed a challenge, but occasionally their adventurous escapades got them into trouble.

When I was three, my older brother, Rex, was sent to take the milk and eggs to market to sell. His older brother, Don, bet him he couldn't drive to the bridge, a half mile away, with his eyes closed. Don promised he'd whistle if Rex started to veer off the road. Rex took the dare, but didn't hear Don whistle—so he careened into a ditch, turning the car on its side. Riding in the back seat, a younger brother and I were not hurt, although we were crying because we were covered with milk and broken eggs. The accident didn't occur because Rex couldn't see—it was because he had his eyes closed.

It is imperative for us to keep our spiritual eyes open. "Watch and pray so that you will not fall into temptation" (Matt. 26:41). We may not fall into a ditch as Rex did, but we are in great danger when we fall into temptation because we've closed our eyes to what God tells us in His Word.

Walk in the Light

Every situation can be a life-lesson if we allow God to teach us. But too often we choose to ignore His wisdom and do what we want. My son, Chip, rented the movie, *Nanny McPhee,* for his family to watch. A few days later, Belle, his four-year-old, threw a walleyed fit. Chip took her on his lap and told her that her behavior was unacceptable. He calmed her a bit and asked, "Belle, do you remember the movie we watched?"

"Yeess."

"Did you see how terrible those children acted until no one wanted to be around them?"

"Uh-huh."

"You don't want to be like that, do you?"

"Nooo."

"Then what do you think you should do about it?"

She wailed, "Not watch the movie!"

We laughed, but it's tragic for those of us who stubbornly refuse to learn the lessons the Lord wants to teach us in life.

An Illuminated Lesson

In a home Bible study one night, we were handed Scriptures relating to light. In the middle of our discussion, the power failed. All the lights in the neighborhood went out. Our host lit a number of candles in the room in order to continue the study.

After about ten minutes, the lights flashed on and someone read the next Scripture: "But if we are living in the light, as God is in the light, then we have fellowship with one another, and the blood of Jesus, his Son, cleanses us from all sin" (1 John 1:7 NLT). The impact of this Scripture gave us goose bumps. The message was clear. God wants us to be a bright reflection of His love by having meaningful relationships.

It's easy to shine and have a wonderful attitude, with love for almost everyone, as long as there's no one else around! But when people come tromping in and say and do things that irritate us, our light may flicker and grow dim. When this happens, it's time to repent, plug in to His power source, and get recharged. The Father commissions us as sons and daughters to be a light—even when we're challenged by other's dark actions and attitudes.

Follow the Star

The Father brought forth the light shining through His Son, to drive back the darkness where the evil one lurks. Jesus was called the Bright and Morning Star. When we follow this Star, as the wise men did, it still leads us to the Messiah. Jesus addressed His followers, "I am the world's Light. No one who follows me stumbles around in the darkness. I provide plenty of light to live in" (John 8:12 MSG). How exciting! When we follow Jesus, the windows of our hearts are scrubbed clean and His incredible light shines through us as we walk along dark valleys.

Gorgeous worldly beauty appears only for a moment before it vanishes or we pass on by. We only retain vague memories of what we see, by attempting to paint mental pictures of each phenomenon.

Although our eyesight fades as we age, the matchless beauty of God's promises become clearer and more vivid as we begin to understand the depth of God's love. He shines on us with all His glory. But we anticipate a time when we'll dwell in the beauty of His presence. His light is bright here, but in eternity His face will be like the noonday sun—too bright for us to look at.

God gave us His Bright and Morning Star as a compass to guide us. During the night, we carefully follow that Star until the day dawns—when we can walk in the full light of the Son. His light glows in our hearts, illuminating hope. Jesus waits to take us by the hand and lead us with insight, even as our physical eyesight begins to fail. Physical eyesight has helped us find our way here, but spiritual insight will help us find our way in the spiritual realm.

Listen carefully. In the midst of all this beauty, we may hear a symphony of praise rising to glorify His name.

Don't be Afraid of the Light

An old house we moved into was infested with cockroaches. Before exterminators came, we'd go in the kitchen at night, turn on the light, and those despicable bugs would scamper everywhere to get out of the light.

The light of God's Word exposes the dark areas of sin, but there's no need to run in fear. God shines the light on our hearts to reveal our sins. He wants to clean us up, so there are no dark smudges to stain our character.

Spiritual light makes our way clear so we don't stumble around in confusion. When we follow the Lord, we move ahead with confidence—walking along the path He lays out for us.

Here on earth, we have the lights God created in the beginning. In heaven, His glory will be the light, and Jesus will be our Lamp. He wants those of us who are His children to be spiritual lights here on earth. We shine as solar-powered energy, absorbing His light in every cell of our body until we glisten from the inside out.

"And so we are transfigured much like the Messiah, our

lives gradually becoming brighter and more beautiful as God enters our lives and we become like him" (2 Cor. 3:18 MSG).

We can sing with Debbie Boone the song she made popular, "You Light up My Life." We take pleasure in lighting up someone's day with godly insight.

The light of His truth leads us to new horizons. In spite of failing physical eyesight, God gives us spiritual insight so we radiate Christlikeness. We open our eyes wide in wonder and expectation as He fills us with light.

At the end of the age, when the world begins to implode, we can count on God's glorious light to *explode*. I envision God sending out His angels to gather those of us who have been His little fireflies and to usher us home into His eternal light. Our light may flicker, like that of a firefly—sometimes on, sometimes off—but hopefully we'll become consistently brighter. "The way of the righteous is like the first gleam of dawn, which shines ever brighter until the full light of day" (Prov. 4:18 NLT). Our whole countenance should begin to light up. Even dim eyes will begin to sparkle.

Remember, as eyesight begins to fail, it's time to ask for *insight.* There's no age limit to become a brighter light than we've dared to believe to lead others to the Father of Light. This becomes a strong encouragement to keep on shining!

LIFE APPLICATION

1. How will spiritual insight lead us to God?
2. How can God's light shine through us as a Christlike example to those around us?
3. Do you blame others or circumstances for the way you act?
4. How does insight differ from head knowledge?
5. How can you gain greater insight?
6. Is there someone in your life who has been a light for you?
7. What can you do to be a light, even to those you're not aware of?
8. Is there any area of your life that hides in darkness?
9. Do you ask God what you're to learn through the difficulties you encounter?
10. How can your light grow brighter as you grow older?

5

CLOUDY VISION AND DARK CIRCUMSTANCES

... and the clouds return after the rain ...
Ecclesiastes 12:2

It seems strange that the wise old king would say clouds come *after* the rain. Typically, clouds roll in before the first sprinkle. Since Solomon's previous statement likely refers to dimming vision, it's possible this phrase is in reference to cataracts that cloud our eyesight as we grow older.

On my last visit to my eye doctor, he told me a cataract in my left eye had reduced my corrected vision to 20/70. He gave me the option of surgery now or waiting. "Let's do it!" I exclaimed. "Not only will I be thrilled to have better vision, but so will all those irritated drivers who've trailed behind me when I've slowed to five miles an hour trying to read street signs."

Psychological Damage Comes After a Storm

We've all seen illustrations of comic strip characters experiencing depression. The posture of these cartoon figures is one of defeat—bent over with gloomy facial expressions, with ominous clouds hovering over them.

When life rains on our parade, dark emotional clouds come

rolling in shortly afterwards. Disappointment punches holes in our reservoir of peace and joy which drains serotonin (good feelings) from our brains. Then, dark clouds move in—heavy with the four dirty Ds: Despair, Despondency, Discouragement, and Depression. These are thundering signals for us to ask God to *reign* over our stormy encounters.

Age offers a broad range of circumstances for psychological attacks. These onslaughts rolling in can be a frightening storm. Memories of bad experiences drift in to haunt us. But we can fight dismal reruns by refusing to replay them. Instead, we're to look for something to bring us joy and distract us. Joy builds a wall of defense against unpleasant memories. My funny bone is usually tickled when watching some of the oldies-but-goodies—reruns of TV comedy episodes—from slapstick to comic relief. Joy, like helium, playfully lifts us above dark clouds.

Answered Prayer

I'd had a rough week. One upsetting thing after another hammered at my peace. I'd had a car accident that was my fault. Then, my computer crashed when I was about two-thirds of the way through the book I was writing, and the geeks couldn't retrieve my manuscript. As the last straw, I stepped on the flash drive and destroyed my backup.

I telephoned my friend, Bette. She didn't answer, but I left a message asking her to pray for me. When she dropped by the house a few hours later, I thanked her for responding to my desperate plea. She said, "I didn't get a call. I just decided to come by." We talked a bit and prayed before she went on her way. My clouded spirit lifted a bit.

That evening I got a phone call from a young man. "My name is not Bette, but I received your call for prayer on my cell phone this morning. I want you to know, I've been praying for you all day. Call me anytime." I swallowed hard, thanked him, and hung up the phone. Had I dialed a wrong number that morning? I don't think so.

We Need Praying Friends

Challenges come with options. We can pace the floor and wring our hands—but in doing so, stress invites self-pity to sit on our shoulder and whisper, "Oh, you poor thing."

This is a time to focus on God, knowing He is still greater than any force coming against us. He can give us the confidence to hold steady, as He gently leads across the shaky bridge to the other side.

Circumstances spell defeat when we allow negative emotions to come puffing in and snuff out glimmers of hope. Clouds of gloom press in, like fog, blocking the vision of the Son. These things make it difficult to make rational decisions. It's hard to pray when we're upset. That's why we need a backup of at least one other person to pray with and for us. "So speak encouraging words to one another. Build up hope so you'll be together on this, no one left out, no one left behind" (1 Thess. 5:11 MSG).

For years my husband, Carey, kept a worn slip of paper in his billfold that read: "Life is what you make it. It isn't so much what happens, but the way in which you take it." We pray for the Holy Spirit to send a gentle breeze of hope and joy to scatter dark thoughts, allowing us to move forward and live godly lives.

When Dark Clouds Hang Low

A young mother, Teresa, attended one of my retreats. Her life had been devastated by grief. Pneumococcal meningitis had taken the life of her little six-year-old daughter.

That weekend, I asked each participant to use materials I'd laid out to make a collage that represented their life. Tears rolled down Teresa's cheeks as she worked on her project. She formed clouds with cotton puffs and drew giant raindrops falling onto a field of brilliant flowers. When she explained her poster to the group, she told us the raindrops represented a rainstorm of tears for her adorable little girl who had died. The beautiful flowers were symbolic of something she hoped would come in spite of her child's death. The group wept with her in her loss.

God never intended for us to squelch our emotions. He gave us tears as an outlet for grief to overflow. Tears may cleanse the soul, but they were never meant to drown our hope.

Teresa experienced some healing as she constructed a poster that symbolically expressed her agony. We hugged her, and in a small way we shared the pain she was going through. She then made a momentous decision. She determined not allow her broken heart to interfere with her being a loving mother for her three other little girls—beautiful flowers, thirsty for loving care. Although agonizing grief stabbed her heart, she would not permit the sorrow to consume her.

Now, several years later, her daughters are blossoming into fine young ladies as the result of her decision. In our suffering, we're not only responsible for our own emotions and grief, but we also need to be aware of how our actions affect those around us.

Empathize with Others

As part of the family of God, we're to reach out with compassion to our brothers and sisters in Christ. Jesus wept with Mary and Martha as they grieved the death of their brother, Lazarus, even though He knew He would soon raise him from the dead. The Lord also tells us to weep with those who weep—to express our loving concern for those who are hurting. "So those who went off with heavy hearts will come home laughing, with armloads of blessing" (Ps. 126:6 MSG).

When bad things happen, we can ask God to breathe on our dying embers of hope and to fan faith into a flame of joyful anticipation. God can strengthen us in our trials to resist being devastated. We find hope when we cling to Almighty God in our valleys of sorrow.

We need to be there for one another. God honors even the small gesture of giving a cup of cold water to someone who is thirsty. Often we comfort others by simply offering them a shoulder to cry on.

We have God's Word to help us hold steady. His wisdom shows us how to handle life when we're up against a wall. We seldom see any purpose in a crisis. There are some situations that happen that we'll never understand this side of heaven. But we pray our loving Father will bring something beneficial to us or to those who watch us. We remind ourselves, "He loves us and cares about every minute detail of our lives."

Jesus set the ultimate example when He held steady in the midst of unimaginable persecution. Dark clouds rolled in as our Lord experienced excruciating pain on the cross. Deep in His heart, however, He held on to tiny scraps of joy. "He was willing to die a shameful death on the cross because of the joy he knew would be his afterwards" (Heb.12:2 TLB).

Birthing New Hope

A woman in labor anticipates a beautiful new baby as a reward for her struggle.

> "When a woman gives birth, she has a hard time, there's no getting around it. But when the baby is born, there is joy in the birth. This precious new life wipes out the debilitating memory of the pain. The sadness you have right now is similar to that pain, but the coming joy is also similar" (John 16:21–22 MSG).

When we are in the midst of misery and pain, God may be giving birth to a new facet of life or a delivery from some sin or addiction.

God observes us carefully in rough times, watching for evidence that we're firmly standing on the Rock. Unlike the foolish man who built his house on the sand, we've made the decision to place our trust in Jesus as our foundation. When the clouds roll in, we're confident we won't drown or be washed away.

Jesus is the silver lining that encircles every dark cloud that looms above the horizon. This silver lining might well represent a doorway of hope. There's an old saying: "Into every life some rain must fall." Without rain, plants won't produce a harvest. We can become strong and fruitful— not *in spite of*, but *because of* the storms

34

we go through. With no challenges, we'd likely grow complacent and take our blessings for granted.

When the children of Israel wandered in the desert for forty years, God sent a cloud to cover them during the day and shelter them from the blistering heat. He never intended for the heat of our trials to destroy us. However, intense heat either hardens or softens. We've been burned by people and circumstances. But we pray those fiery trials will soften our hearts and keep them pliable enough for God to continue to mold us.

Don't Let Dark Clouds Produce Dark Moods

God reigns down righteousness when we refuse to let troubles and trials ruin our walk with Him. A godly focus gives us victory when we refuse to allow dark clouds to be the source of dark moods. "Sing to God, sing in praise of his name, extol him who rides on the clouds; rejoice before him—his name is the LORD" (Ps. 68:4).

In the middle of our personal storms, wisdom allows us to see beyond our pain, realizing His creative plan still shines above those clouds. Wisdom would have us look up, knowing He is greater than any and all circumstances. Praise His Holy Name!

Clouds provide protection, as well as refreshing rain. The clean, fresh smell of the earth after the rain delights us because we know the seeds we've planted will soon be sprouting. Patience and faithfulness produce a bumper crop when we stand strong during storms. We're blessed, and we bless others as we hold steadfast.

Jesus Is Coming Soon

At the end of the age, when Jesus returns in the clouds, it may be a dark day when angry clouds make us feel fearful and helpless. Jesus has promised to break through those clouds with shouts of victory over every evil force.

Indeed, the return of Jesus will come with power beyond description. "They will see the Son of Man coming on the clouds of the sky, with power and great glory" (Mark 13:26). This wondrous and victorious picture of Jesus ruling and reigning over every principality, power, and dark evil of this world gives us peace and pure delight.

When that great day comes, every eye will behold Him and every knee will bow. Everyone will know without a doubt He is the Lord of lords and the King of kings. Suddenly, the light of revelation will burst forth, and people of every tribe, tongue, and nation will see that He has been there all along—watching and walking us triumphantly through every stage of life. The enemy is defeated. Praise God, He's coming again!

LIFE APPLICATION

1. How can you keep your attitude right when everything seems to be going wrong?
2. Talk about any bad memory that still plagues you.
3. What negative emotions arise when things don't go as you want?
4. How do you handle negative emotions?
5. Are you aware of how your bad mood affects those around you?
6. What value are tears?
7. What makes you laugh?
8. Do you ever blame God when things go wrong?
9. How might Satan defeat you when you're experiencing trouble?
10. How can you look beyond your troubles?

6
ALL SHOOK UP

... when the keepers of the house tremble ...
Ecclesiastes 12:3

With the onset of age, it's not uncommon for Parkinson's disease or general weaknesses to cause people to shake or tremble. Handwriting may become less legible. And since doctors already have the reputation of poor handwriting, pity the poor pharmacists who attempt to read an *older* doctor's prescriptions.

Linda took her five-year-old, Betsy, to see her Aunt Sue who had advanced Parkinson's disease. Driving home, Betsy said, "Mom, we need to pray for Aunt Sue.

"That's a great idea. Remind me tonight and we'll do that."

"But we need to pray for her to get saved."

"Honey, Aunt Sue has been a Christian for years."

"Then we need to pray she becomes a better Christian."

Linda whirled around to face Betsy. "What in the world are you talking about?"

Eyes wide with childish innocence, Betsy explained, "Well, our memory verse in class yesterday was, "The righteous will never be shaken.""

This verse is a reminder—we're not to be shaken on the inside, even when we tremble on the outside. Fear often causes people to shake. Though fear is a God-given emotion, it seems to have been originally designed for flight or fight. Since we aren't in the fleeing or fighting mode much these days, this stuffed energy flutters around inside as free-floating anxiety and interferes with our thinking and performance.

Fears Can Immobilize

Even after I became an adult, ominous threats of danger seemed to lurk around every dark corner. Quite possibly, the problem began as a child when I listened to scary radio programs. (Does that date me or what?) One ongoing serial was called *Inner Sanctum Mystery.* Chills ran down my spine when the program began with a door squeaking open and then closing with a heavy thud. My friends and I told spooky stories and went to horror movies. We pushed the limit by going to the cemetery to tell ghost stories. After a while, fear became my constant companion, haunting me everywhere I went.

A limb scratching the screen at night would grab my attention and scare me spitless. I was convinced something or someone was crawling into my dark bedroom. My trembling and racing heart was every bit as affected as if some monster was actually coming to devour me. Imagination, added to fear, led to panic.

I prayed God would give me the ability to reel in my wild fears. It took years of prayer for me to truly accept God's ever-present protection. He is aware of everything His children are going through. I reminded myself of Jesus' promise—to leave us a peace beyond anything the world ever experienced. "Peace I leave with you; my peace I give you. I do not give to you as the world gives" (John 14:27).

This sounded good, but I realized I had the responsibility to slam the door and refuse to surround myself with fearful distractions. I knew if I kept recycling terrifying thoughts, these would chisel a chink in my armor and allow fear to wreak havoc with my emotions. To this day, I refuse to watch horror movies or violent television shows.

Worry Is an Off-shoot of Fear

In my early years of marriage, an aspect of fear turned into worry. Carey once told me, "When you don't have enough to worry about, you'll look for someone else with problems to help them worry." I hated to admit it, but he was right. I'd wring my hands with anxiety and rub fearful possibilities between my fingers. When I made an attempt to give my anxiety to God, He seemed to whisper, "If you'll get your grubby little hands off, I'll take care of things."

Carey traveled, and sometimes he'd be late coming home. A few times, my worrisome fears escalated until I'd call the highway department to see if any wrecks had been reported on his route. One dreary night, as I paced the floor, I planned his funeral and decided what I'd wear on that fateful day! I later repented for my lack of faith. As I continued to pray, destructive worries began to fade. *Thank You, Lord. In time, you lowered my anxiety level until it fell within normal limits.*

Inordinate anxiety is the springboard to worry and fear. It is accompanied with a passel of apprehensions, distresses, and dread. Satan edges in with tidbits of these *hors d'oeuvres,* and every chance he gets, he serves us a whole platter of fear.

Fear is not only dangerous—it's also contagious. When people around us pick up on our fears, it can easily escalate to mob reaction. The Word teaches us we can come against this instigator of terror by humbly coming before God to enlist His power to resist the devil. Only His authority can force the enemy to back off.

Find Some Distraction

When the planes crashed into the Twin Towers, Linda called her husband repeatedly at work to inform him of the latest details. She stayed glued to the TV, watching the replays of the collapsing buildings. Anxiety escalated. Finally, her husband said, "Linda, do us both a favor and turn off the TV. Find something to distract you so you're not consumed by this tragedy."

Worry drains us physically. Most of us would rather scrub floors or dig ditches, rather than be locked in a cage where worry eats away at our peace. Instead, we can huddle closer to God. "God is a safe place to hide, ready to help when we need Him. We stand fearless at the cliff-edge of doom, courageous in sea-storm and earthquake, before the rush and roar of oceans, the tremors that shift mountains" (Ps. 46:1–3 MSG). Only the Lord can infuse us with enough peace to stop trembling.

Worry does nothing to help solve a problem—it compounds it. I lost five members of my family in four years. For a while, each time the phone jangled, I jumped. I was afraid something had happened to another loved one. We nurture seeds of worrisome thoughts by watering them with a list of *what-ifs*. This causes them to sprout and grow and affect every aspect of our lives.

Learn to Hold Steady Facing Small Things

God often builds our emotional immune system by inoculating us with small doses of challenges. Even simple things like traffic, waiting for a doctor's report, or looking for lost keys can send us into a tizzy. When we learn to deal with small things, bigger problems often become manageable. We take as our motto an old saying, "Yard by yard, life is hard, but inch by inch, life's a cinch." Our goal is to come to the point where we can exclaim, "When besieged, I'm calm as a baby. When all hell breaks loose, I'm collected and cool" (Ps. 27:3 MSG).

Hold Steady in the Moment

When I had my first child, Kathy, I decided to use the then little-known method of natural childbirth. I'd read some articles and a "how-to" book on relaxing, exercise, and proper breathing.

With my doctor's consent, I followed each step as labor progressed. I concentrated on staying calm, taking one contraction at a time—breathing, relaxing, and watching the clock. I determined each minute would accomplish its purpose in bringing me closer to delivery.

Nurses couldn't understand my composure. However, I didn't have to wonder why they called it labor; it *was* hard work.

This taught me the value of living in the peace and the power of the present moment. This discipline prepared me for other struggles in life—dealing with life one small step at a time.

There Are Valid Concerns

Carey had gone to the hospital for tests. Rectal bleeding had been a concern. He called me on the phone. His fearful words were barely audible. "It's cancer."

I gasped. "I'll be right there." I cradled the phone slowly on its base as shock and sorrow rose from my heart until they reached my eyes and spilled over in the form of tears. I called a friend who rushed over and offered a shoulder to cry on. She shook me gently. "Cry your eyes out on the way to the hospital, but pull yourself together before going into his room."

I followed her advice and paused momentarily outside Carey's door to take a deep breath and utter a quick prayer. Going near his bedside, I faked confidence. "Hey, Tiger, it looks like we have a battle on our hands. We're in this fight together and by God's grace, we'll win this war." Day after day, we determined to face the future by only dealing with the battle of the day.

Science has proven that worry and anxiety lower the immune system as well as damage us emotionally and spiritually. After Carey's diagnosis, I periodically fought headaches and an upset stomach, to the point of being nauseous.

Tension caused me to make mistakes on my job. Fear revved the engines of my nervous system until I was exhausted. Like a sponge, it sopped up my energy, wrung me out, and left me limp. Carey's concern involved a fight for his life. My battles were emotional. I fought against fearful attacks that stemmed from bad news. Day after day, God taught me to sit down and untangle the knots of yesterday's problems that threatened to keep me tied up with fear.

I refused to get bound up with tomorrow's dark threats. Friends offered appropriate scriptures to help me see life from God's perspective. Tunnel vision became a friend by helping me concentrate on the one problem I faced at the moment. Like the old-fashioned blinders on a horse, I kept focused on what lay directly ahead. The Lord's faithfulness held me steady as Carey's health deteriorated.

In facing the challenge, Carey and I attempted to live in day-tight compartments—closing the doors behind us to protect us from yesterday's battles. We kept future doors locked, knowing threats of pain and death mocked on the other side.

I made a commitment to Carey that whatever time we had together, we'd make the best of it. I made a conscious effort to do things that pleased him. It made me wonder, "Why did I wait for disaster before searching for special things to bring him joy?"

We can choose to run to God immediately when worry plagues us. We remind ourselves that He alone can infuse us with the courage to hold on to Him as He soothes our anxieties and helps control our shaking.

The Future Is in God's Hand

Most of us have concerns about growing older. When I lost my retirement money by putting it in a bad investment, I was afraid my money would expire before I did. When diseases and disabilities showed up in my peers, my own concerns mounted. When I lost things or forgot something, I'd wonder if it was the onset of Alzheimer's. (The thing I'd miss the most is losing my mind!)

It saddens and discourages me to lose older friends and loved ones through death. The problem is obvious when I go to a family or high school reunion and am aware of the shrinking numbers. We're forced to face our own mortality. We pray God will not allow this to shake us or make us fearful.

We must refuse to open a Pandora's box of imaginary demons

that can torment us. We must depend on God to show us how to slam the lid shut and trust Him.

> "David said it all: 'I saw God before me for all time. Nothing can shake me; he's right by my side. I'm glad from the inside out, ecstatic; I've pitched my tent in the land of hope'" (Acts 2:25–26 MSG).

Hold steady, friend. Almighty God is our blessed hope.

Godly Concerns

Reasonable concern over any situation is healthy. God intended for us to use common sense as a protection. A police officer spoke at a meeting I attended and told us to never ignore gut-level feelings of caution. He said, "Many who ignore such warnings suffer dire consequences."

Especially as we mature as Christians, it is essential for us to listen to God rather than reacting to our emotions. Emotions tend to act as a hook, snagging us in the jaw and dragging us around. We build confidence in the One who is the epitome of strength and peace. He invites us to enter into His rest.

God gives us opportunities not only to accept the challenges of this stage of life—He has also equipped us with the ability to adapt. When I find myself feeling shaky, Psalm 91 helps me hunker down and stand strong as fears assault. It would be good to memorize this chapter to quote when we're surrounded by trouble.

Benefits of a Calm Spirit

When we're at peace, we're able to think more creatively. Fresh ideas often pop into my mind when I'm falling asleep, during the night, or early in the morning. New and creative ideas flicker across my brain, like clicking the remote to a new TV channel. Calm composure sets the climate for creative thinking.

I've heard of some who wake up in the night with a new song lilting across their consciousness. An acquaintance dreamed of a unique invention for which he later got a patent.

Some keep a flashlight and notepad by their bed to write down new ideas that drift through their minds during the night. Perhaps that's the reason we should sleep on a decision before acting on it. Rest has a way of ushering us into the presence of a creative God. His voice is never clearer than when our minds are at peace. "Be still, and know that I am God" (Ps. 46:10).

Philippians contains the powerful prerequisite to peace. "Do not be anxious about anything, but in everything, by prayer and petition, with thanksgiving, present your requests to God. And the peace of God that transcends all understanding will guard your hearts and your minds in Christ Jesus" (Phil. 4:6–7). We wrap and seal a large package of prayer with gratitude and thanksgiving.

Have you ever noticed how much easier it is to remain at peace in the midst of praise and worship? I know of groups in a foreign country that worship in house churches where their services are sometimes broken into by the authorities. Once, a gang burst into a worship service breaking things and beating the members. The Christians began to sing louder. This so frustrated the assailants, they stormed out of the meeting place. Those Christians remained unflappable.

As a strange response, the leader of the gang called the church a few weeks later and said, "Could some of us start coming to church there? Christianity is so much different from what we thought." As a result, some of those same gang members became believers.

God Is Always Aware

It's wonderful that God is not only aware of the mounds of worrisome dirt in our lives, but He is also concerned with the dust particles of anxieties and apprehensions sprinkled throughout our day.

We Christians fight an ongoing spiritual war with the devil. Our battles are often fierce, when the enemy comes with a barrage of problems to shake us up with wave after wave of attacks. But it is possible to remain calm if we predetermine God is our strong defense.

Combating Fear

Think of the acronym: **F**ear is **E**vidence that **A**ppears **R**eal. Fear is stirred up by imagining potential dangers. President Roosevelt, in his fireside chats during World War II, reminded his listeners, "The only thing to fear is fear itself."

Our minds cannot focus on two different things at the same time. Our fears begin to evaporate when we are confident of God's wisdom and power, rather than assuming we only have our own resources to rely on. Our Lord is there to defend and hold us in His righteous right hand. I feel safer when someone strong holds my hand. *Ah, thanks, that's much better.*

It's time to pitch our tents in the land of hope. The God of love rules over this spiritual kingdom where we live. His love casts out fear. Our Heavenly Father is our homeland security. Neither terror nor dreads hold office in His house of representatives. Fear wields no power in His regime.

Our Heavenly Father is our Jehovah Nissi, our banner. We lift Him up in a land where we remain confident and composed. His flag is never lowered to half mast, signifying death or defeat. We raise it higher, rather than lower, during the storms of life.

LIFE APPLICATION

1. How can a Christian hold steady during difficult times?
2. Is there an area of emotional weakness in your life?
3. Can you graciously accept physical weakness as a part of aging?
4. Are you concerned or fearful about the future?
5. Do you spend too much time worrying about who will take care of you in later years?
6. Is it difficult for you to go to sleep at night because of anxiety?
7. Do you know how to take your thoughts captive?
8. Can you trust God to bring good things from bad situations?
9. Do you ever take time to sit and think creatively—to write a poem, play or sing a song, or think about what heaven will be like?
10. Can you think of creative ways to reach out to others?

7

WEAK BONES AND HEAVY LOADS

... the strong men stoop ...
Ecclesiastes 12:3

Osteoporosis often causes older people to stoop. It advances as subtly as a mouse nibbling away at cheese in a trap. We often notice the problem in others before we're aware of our own hunching shoulders. My doctor told me I had the beginnings of osteoporosis and recommended I take some medication. I suppose I will. Refusing to take the meds might imply I'm stup-id—and as a result, I'd end up stoop-ed.

My brother, Don, was never tall. As he grew older and lost bone density, he also lost precious inches. When a friend made fun of his short stature, his wife, Mickey, spoke proudly, "He's about the biggest man I know." Don's integrity and strength of character explained why she felt he stood head and shoulders above most men. Regardless of a person's physical height or feelings of insignificance, one can still stand tall in God's sight.

Other Reasons for Stooping

Some older people stoop and drag around as if they question whether they're worth anything anymore. Somewhat like termites eating away at the structure of a house, lack of purpose chomps away at their feelings of significance. Upbeat attitudes are apt to crumble and leave one pathetically bent over. We need God, as the Great Exterminator, to destroy these enemies of our soul.

Jesus spoke to those carrying heavy burdens.

> "Come to me, all of you who are tired and have heavy loads, and I will give you rest. ... I am gentle and humble in spirit, and you will find rest for your lives. The burden that I ask you to accept is easy; the load I give you to carry is light" (Matt. 11:28–30 NCV).

Our gracious older Brother also encourages us to cast our cares on Him. (I must admit, "I believe I need casting lessons.")

How to Handle Discouragement

It takes commitment to stay optimistic when the cares of the world overwhelm us. Rather than whimper and complain, we must look to God. He sent His Son, empowered by the Holy Spirit, to give us strength and encouragement. He lifts us up when we've been beaten down.

Satan, the father of lies, taunts us in an attempt to make us feel weak and useless. Though we aren't as strong as we were when we were young, God gives us the strength and ability to do everything He commissioned us to do—even in the latter stages of life.

As years go by, when our strength and energy begin to wane, God invites us to lean more heavily on Him. "Trust in GOD. Lean on your God!" (Isa. 50:10 MSG).

When we mope around with our attitudes bent out of shape, we're a poor witness for Christianity. Instead, we can stand proud—proclaiming what God has done for us throughout our lives. With the Lord's strength coursing through our veins, we are able to straighten up in God's bright presence to worship our Messiah, Jesus, in all His majesty and power.

We're of Value at Every Age

Growing older may be like a crucible, testing how steadfast we'll stand as the ravages of time pummel our bodies. They no longer look, feel, or function as they did when we were young. But we can depend on God's promises and remain spiritually anchored, even when our bodies drift about aimlessly.

Centuries ago, older people sat in the marketplace, to share with those passing by. An Old Testament prophet foretold, "Once again men and women of ripe old age will sit in the streets of Jerusalem, each with cane in hand because of his age"(Zech. 8:4). Note that Zechariah talked about a *cane* in their hand, but not sitting on their *can*. They sat there to *give out* rather than looking for *a hand out*.

Leaning on God

Some accuse believers of using Christianity as a crutch. I do! I lean heavily on that staff with no apologies. Not only would I stoop, but without Him to hold me steady, I'd fall flat on my face. I'm thankful He keeps me standing strong.

When we wander off the narrow way, God comes looking for us. Jesus is pictured as the Shepherd searching for lost sheep—those of us who have strayed. He binds up our wounds and carries us when we are weary. When I'm weary and bent down, I like to think of Jesus picking me up and hoisting me onto His shoulders.

We're to Continue to Carry a Load

This is neither a time for us to become freeloaders nor collapse in an easy chair expecting everyone to wait on us. We're not to send out invitations to a pity party where we whine: "I've taken care of everyone else—now it's time for others to look after me."

Complacency isn't a godly characteristic. Our Creator designed us to carry our share of the load for as long as we're here. The stronger are to carry heavier burdens, while those of us who are weaker may carry less. Everyone is to be involved.

It's good to periodically take note of what we've been assigned to carry. When our strength and energy begin to wane, we may need to let go of some tasks we've taken on. It's important to know where our responsibility should end and the responsibility of others should kick in. God's wisdom helps us adapt to those changes. The Lord would have us be aware what we need to hang onto and what we're to let go.

Handicaps from Birth or Injuries

Nick Vujicic, a young man from Australia, was born with no arms or legs—a condition with no medical explanation. Yet he travels worldwide, spreading his message of hope and encouragement. He has a powerful DVD called *Life Without Limbs—From No Limbs to No Limits.* In this video, he explains how his handicap has become an asset, rather than a liability.

In his early years, he fought depression and would have dared to take his life. But he laughs and says, "Without arms or legs, how in the world could I do myself in?" His parents, faced with Nick's debilitating handicap, struggled to maintain an unwavering faith. When they accepted the fact that there was no way to correct his problem, they worked with him to help him become as independent as possible.

Nick has a little flipper off his hip with a couple of toe-like appendages protruding. With those, he can type forty words a minute. With great tenacity, faith, and a sense of humor, he accomplishes unimaginable tasks.

Now, he thanks God for his body. Because of his unusual disability, thousands come to hear him tell his story and preach the Good News of Jesus. God opens doors for him in countries and places inaccessible to most Christians. When he speaks of the abundant life he's found, people listen with rapt attention and are amazed at his peace and joy. He not only accepts his body, but his commitment has opened the door for him to take advantage of God-given opportunities to spread the gospel through his unusual outreach. He gives the glory to his Heavenly Father. His shoulders don't slump, and he refuses to allow his spirit to stoop.

The strongest man in the world appears weak compared to Nick, who has overcome incomprehensible difficulties through his faith in God.

> "My grace is enough; it's all you need. My strength comes into its own in your weakness. ... Now I take limitations in stride, and with good cheer, these limitations that cut me down to size—abuse, accidents, opposition, bad breaks. I just let Christ take over! And so the weaker I get, the stronger I become" (2 Cor. 12:9–10 MSG).

There are others who are handicapped as the result of accidents. Joni Erickson Tada became a quadriplegic as the result of a swimming mishap. As a beautiful teenager, she dove in the water, hit bottom, and broke her neck. Although she is unable to use her limbs, she has touched the lives of people around the world. She explains how dogged determination and her faith in God have allowed her to do far more than anyone ever expected. She's a talented vocalist, an author, and a motivational speaker. She developed her remarkable artistic talent by drawing with a paint brush clenched between her teeth.

In the light of these two incredibly strong Christians, the excuses I use for not staying upbeat with a few stumbling blocks of aging are pathetic.

The Plight of a Retiring Athlete

Imagine an older athlete entering the locker room for the last time to hang up his jersey. For years, he's received his self-worth from cheering crowds. As he stands there now, his shoulders may droop as he chokes back the tears. He realizes other athletes have stood where he now stands, but this gives him little comfort. Discouragement may sweep over him when realizes he will no longer be the star of the game. It may cause him to feel weak and inadequate.

However, if he decides to become a star in God's sight, he can envision the Lord standing and shouting His approval, cheering him on. Rather than a hero in the sports world, he can accept God's offer to be drafted into another race where he'll never need to step down because of age, disability, or lack of strength. He'll never sit on the sidelines as a substitute, wishing he were on the playing field. He has been called by God to stay in the game—to win the championship game of life.

A wise, retired athlete refuses to remain stuck, finding only bits of comfort from his past accolades. His reward comes as he realizes it's not a gold medal that's most important, but rather a golden crown. He knows there's a gold welcome mat laid out before him in heaven.

> "You've all been to the stadium and seen the athlete's race. Everyone runs; one wins. Run to win. All good athletes train hard. They do it for a gold medal that tarnishes and fades. You're after one that's gold eternally" (1 Cor. 9:24–25 MSG).

In the Christian race, God has made it possible for all participants to be winners, regardless of age or natural abilities. God gives each of us the strength to finish the race.

It is wise to wrap the gift of today in blessings and encouragement and offer it to those around us in order that they might have a better tomorrow. Not only will this help others stand tall, but we will also find ourselves standing straight and strong. As we encourage others, we too become encouraged.

Don't Fall into the Trap of Complaining

A bad attitude is worse than any physically debilitating handicap. Sour attitudes are exhibited by far too many people when they face the impositions of aging. I have to admit, it is disturbing to have Father Time hacking away at health and energy, but we have the choice as to how we will respond.

An older church member in Idaho constantly complained about

his health—his arthritis, a headache, a bellyache, and his lack of energy. He even added to the list—poor finances, bad crops, and unappreciative children. The more he talked, the more his shoulders drooped.

Carey listened to him until he'd had enough. One Sunday, after listening to this man's laundry list of gripes, Carey looked the grumpy man in the eye. "Brother, I'm going to keep asking you how you feel until one day you'll tell me you're feeling good."

The old man shook his head and moaned, "I never will." He'd made the decision to never change his attitude. How sad when our focus is on everything that's wrong with life.

When we continue to complain, we're likely to drag down others who are within earshot. The more we talk about our problems, the worse it makes us feel as well as those who have to listen to us.

My sister attends church where a woman is actually bent double. She has difficulty getting around, even with a walker. However, as she twists her head to look up, she has a radiant smile and speaks to everyone she meets. Her body is stooped, but not her spirit.

God Doesn't Expect More than We are Able to Do

As a teen, I was a fair athlete and would attempt most anything on a dare. Now that I'm older, I admit my limitations and back away from tasks God hasn't assigned to me.

> "I have strength for all things in Christ who empowers me. I am ready for anything and equal to anything through Him who infuses inner strength into me; I am self-sufficient in Christ's sufficiency" (Phil. 4:13 AMP).

God isn't so interested in our jumping high hurdles or knocking a ball out of the park, but He expects us to follow through with what He has planned for us. It may well be the last inning of the game, but when He pitches the ball, He intends for us to at least take a swing at it. He brings out the very best in us and will be our coach until the end of the game.

The Danger of Falling

As a person grows older, there's not only the tendency to stoop, but also a danger of falling. We are wise when we take precautions to keep safe.

Spiritually, we must also commit to hold steady and not fall away from the Lord.

> "And now to him who can keep you on your feet, standing tall in his bright presence, fresh and celebrating—to our one God, our only Savior, through Jesus Christ our Master, be glory, majesty and strength and rule before all time and now, and to the end of time. Yes" (Jude vv. 24–25 MSG).

During our latter years, we can choose to be a blessing rather than a burden. Even if we should become totally helpless and have to be cared for, we won't be an unbearable burden as long as we refuse to grumble, complain, or gripe. If we were flat on our backs, we'd still have the option of remaining pleasant, peaceful, and prayerful, rather than pitiful, pathetic, and pessimistic.

Physical strength will fail after a time, but spiritual and emotional strength can grow stronger every day. In the meantime—and it may well be a *mean time*—we can lift others up rather than drag them down.

LIFE APPLICATION

1. What does it mean for one to stand tall spiritually?
2. How do you cast your cares on the Lord?
3. Have you ever viewed aging as a test?
4. Are you shouldering a load that should be someone else's responsibility?
5. Can you think of someone who has an incredible attitude in spite of a great handicap?
6. Who has been a positive influence on you as they grew older?
7. Do your thoughts radiate optimism or pessimism?
8. Have you made the choice to be a blessing at this point in time?
9. Are there times when you've been tempted to give up, throw up your hands, and give in to discouragement?
10. Do you ask the Lord to guide you in all your ways and leave tomorrow in His hands?

8

I CAN CHEW ON IDEAS WITHOUT TEETH

... the grinders cease because they are few ...
Ecclesiastes 12:3

No doubt Solomon referred to the golden-agers losing their teeth. It's not uncommon for people to begin to lose some or all their teeth as they grow older. I felt bad when Dad lost his teeth because of a gum disease. All I could say was, "Well, Dad . . . gum it!"

Tooth or Consequences?

Dentists have looked in my mouth and said, "It looks like you've spent a lot of time in a dentist's chair." They're right, and on some of those visits, I've had experiences I'd rather forget. One dentist told me he might break my jaw when he attempted to pull impacted wisdom teeth. He didn't break my jaw, but my hair stood on end when he said, "Don't worry, I invented a special tool for this kind of job. I call it my crow bar!" Another dentist broke a drill bit off in a root canal procedure. Thank goodness, he got the bit out. I'm still grateful we have good dentists who help us keep our *grinders.*

While I was teaching in prison, a prisoner squinted and asked, "Would you open your mouth?"

"Why?"

"You've got a lot of gold in there."

I closed my mouth quickly, not daring to think what he wanted to do. "Oh, not that much," I mumbled and quickly changed the subject.

I once fell and knocked my bottom teeth back and pushed the top teeth up in my gums. The orthodontist repositioned my teeth and wired them together. I assumed I'd lose weight, but found I could suck more calories through a straw than most people can shovel in with a spoon. Grinding ceased for a while, while the food chain only dropped to a simpler level. But I could still chew on decisions without discomfort.

Some Have No Food to Chew On

God commissioned us to feed the hungry. Grinding ceases for some, not because of lack of teeth, but because there's nothing to eat.

When we lived in Denver and our children were three, two, and six months old, we received a call asking if we could take in four children whose mother had deserted them. They ranged in age from two weeks to five years old.

We arrived at the concrete-block shell of a home and went in. The smell of filth and burned oatmeal caused us to gag. We placed our hands over our noses and mouths. The gaunt father stood in the doorway hanging his head. "I can't take care of them anymore. That burnt oatmeal on the stove is all we've had to eat the past three days."

We gathered the children and got them in the car. The two older ones pressed their little noses against the car window and waved to their daddy until he was out of sight. We drove home in silence. There, I discovered the baby's diaper hadn't been changed for so long it had to be soaked off with warm water. I watched in horror as blood oozed to the surface of her tender bottom. The tiny child whimpered, too weak to cry. She could take no more than one or two ounces of milk until her stomach expanded to normal size.

When I opened a jar of junior baby food for the eleven-month-old, the five-year-old snatched the lid and licked it. Then I began to peel carrots for supper. She grabbed the peelings off the counter and stuffed them in her mouth. My heart ached. I'd never seen starving children before.

We kept them a few weeks until arrangements were made for these little ones to be adopted. Their mother signed the papers to give them up. She never came to see them or tell them good-bye. My sister-in-law, Helen, was thrilled beyond words to adopt the three-year-old boy and the tiny baby girl.

When leaving for their new homes, their little faces were shining and their hair squeaky clean. They were excited and happy. They'd never be abandoned again. Never again would they live in filth or experience the gnawing hunger pains.

The Spiritually Hungry Need Food

A reporter interviewed a street person on TV—a woman who lived under a bridge. She smiled a toothless grin and said, "Let me show you my house of praise." She led the reporter under a bridge and showed him a cardboard structure she'd built to sleep in. Her grinders were few, but obviously the woman's spiritual hunger was satisfied by glorifying God.

There are the multitudes of spiritually malnourished, even among the rich. Many have a hunger in their hearts, a longing for something more. God wants to fill that emptiness with Himself, to nourish their souls with the whipped cream of blessings, sweetened with encouragement, and a cherry of love plopped on top.

Jesus—the Bread of Life

Jesus was born in a village called Bethlehem, which means "house of bread." There, Mary placed Him in a bed—a feed trough in a stable. In His adult ministry, He proclaimed, "I am the bread that gives life! No one who comes to me will ever be hungry. No one who has faith in me will ever be thirsty" (John 6:35 CEV).

After Jesus fasted for forty days in the wilderness, the devil tempted Him by reminding Him that He could turn the stones to bread. Jesus didn't hesitate. He confronted the evil one: "It is written, man does not live on bread alone'" (Luke 4:4). Jesus let him know He had come to do exactly as He and His Father planned.

What We Eat and Why We Eat

I enjoy eating. I eat to celebrate. I eat when I'm depressed. I eat to be sociable, and I eat when I'm bored. *Bon appétit.* I hope the Philippians 3:19 that reads "Their God is their belly" wasn't written to condemn me. I'll admit, there's a temptation to stuff my stomach and placate my conscience with the resolution to, "Eat, drink, and be merry, for tomorrow I diet."

In the abundance of our economy many have become picky eaters. I have little patience with those who only eat meat and potatoes or refuse to eat leftovers. Jesus reminded us, "Don't fuss about what's on the table at mealtimes or whether the clothes in your closet are in fashion. There is far more to your life than the food you put in your stomach, more to your outer appearance than the clothes you hang on your body" (Matt. 6:25 MSG).

The shelves in most of our pantries and refrigerators are stocked with many choices of food. Often, I stand in front of the refrigerator with the door open. I'm not especially hungry, but looking to see if there's anything that appeals to my taste buds.

Be Aware of What Others Need

Instead of looking for what I need, it's time to pay attention to what others need. I could live for a period of time without buying groceries. As we consider third world countries, there are many who need food or clean water in order to survive. We can buy or take food to the hungry, as well as help stock food banks and give clothing to those shivering from the cold in our area.

Christians are to be known as people who feed the hungry, give water to the thirsty, and find homes for the homeless. They go to visit the shut-ins and those in prison.

I pray we're more interested in reaching out to others in need rather than worrying about what we're going to wear to social gatherings, or where we're going to go out to eat. Many in our affluent society have allowed material possessions to become the most important thing in their lives.

I was shocked when a Christian woman from a foreign country visited my home. She sat down to eat, looked around and marveled, "It must be so hard to be a Christian here. You have so many things to distract you."

A Spunky Little Irishman

Eddie Grindley came from Ireland as a young boy. He went to Los Angeles, where he worked in a hotel as a bellhop. He lived an ungodly life—drinking, gambling, stealing, and doing whatever he wanted.

A pretty young lady, Stella, was the elevator operator at the same hotel where he worked. Eddie kept asking her for a date. She refused to go out with him until he agreed to go with her to worship. Since he had no other option, he reluctantly followed her to church.

Eddie fell in love with Stella and with her Lord. His conversion so impacted him, he went out to find others who lived under bridges and in the slums. He identified with the smelly, hungry, winos, and indigent. He marched them down the aisles of the church to seat them on the front pews. Some members were repulsed and indignant. They tried to discourage Eddie, or at least have him seat these derelicts on back rows. But Eddie was undaunted.

He was exuberant when many of the street people were converted to Christ and their spiritual hunger was totally satisfied. Jesus became their Bread of Life. The church members were amazed as they saw the Word of God transform many of these men and women until they became strong members of the body of Christ. Some found jobs and transitioned back into society. Happily, they became incredible examples of the transforming power of the gospel.

However, there were others who only came for a handout. Still, Eddie fed and clothed them. If those invited to the spiritual feast weren't filled, it was because they refused to come to the Lord's Table and eat.

Don't Ignore the Invitation

Jesus talked about the socially prominent being invited to a banquet. When the day of the occasion arrived, they weaseled out. Justifiably angry over their refusal to come, the host sent for those out on the highways and byways to come enjoy his banquet. The King of kings goes to great lengths to prepare for His guests. When people blow Him off, it makes him angry and He extends His invitation to bring in anyone who wants a square meal. He blesses the misfits and the homeless by offering them the feast of a lifetime.

Some treat the Lord's invitation like trash, tossing it out with the junk mail. "That's what I mean when I say, 'Many get invited; only a few make it'" (Matt. 22:14 MSG). How exciting to look forward to sitting down at His banquet table in heaven. He can seat us wherever He chooses.

Communion

At the Last Supper, Jesus took the bread, offered thanks, and gave it to his disciples, telling them it was His body. After that, He took the cup and told them it was His blood of the covenant, which He offered for many. Communion gives us the blessed privilege of Jesus becoming more a part of who we are. This is a time for us to bond with Jesus, as well as with fellow believers. There's a Hebrew expression of *l'chaim*—to life! This becomes a toast as we eat the bread and drink the fruit of the vine. We celebrate this wondrous life-sustaining occasion.

A Hunger for God

I prayed for a fresh infilling of the Holy Spirit and found myself devouring Scripture and chewing on the meat of His Word. I picked up the Bible, not just out of habit, but with a yearning to know more about the Author. Reading the Bible was no longer a matter of checking off another item on my to-do list. Rather, this moved to my top priority.

There's no need for us to be content with crumbs— the bits and pieces of God's Word we pick up attending church on Sunday morning. Jesus told us we are to live by every word that comes from the mouth of God. This challenges me to stop picking and choosing those things that suit my fancy. The things I've underlined in my Bible are not the only important issues.

As we study more of God's Word, we see Him at work all around us. Maturity doesn't come from a quick snack, but rather from eating a full meal. "You're blessed when you've worked up a good appetite for God. He's food and drink in the best meal you'll ever eat" (Matt. 5:6 MSG). The Word of God does much more than fill our belly when we hunger and thirst for righteousness.

Our digestive system is designed to rid our bodies of waste— things that are counter-productive to good health. Spiritually, we need to rid our lives of those things that are damaging to our spiritual health—things like malice, pride, hatred, and selfishness.

We all need God-given nourishment. His special food is like an antioxidant that destroys every demon-induced virus. Our spiritual immune system wards off anger, resentment, and unforgiveness. His Word will make us healthy inside and out.

What a joy to know we can take our everyday, ordinary life of eating, sleeping, and working to please God. *I ain't much, Lord, but I hear you sometimes delight in picking the unlikely. We're all we've got. If you have something in mind for us, have at it! Since you adopted us as your children, we're ready to accept whatever You place in front of us on the table. Keep us from turning up our noses at anything You put on our plates.*

Preparing for the Last Journey

We may not be ready to pack our bags yet, but travel brochures advertising our heavenly home are exciting. It will be God's choice of timing. "Compared to what's coming, living conditions around here seem like a stopover in an unfurnished shack and we're tired of it! We've been given a glimpse of the real thing, our true home in our resurrection bodies! "The Spirit of God whets our appetite by giving us a taste of what's ahead. He puts a little of heaven in our hearts so that we'll never settle for less" (2 Cor. 5:5 MSG). Jesus, as our Bread of Life, keeps us well-nourished and fit for the journey ahead.

Our mouths may water as we anticipate the feast God is preparing for us. He's given us some appetizers for us to "taste and see that He is good." I know He'll prepare the greatest banquet we've ever attended. I anticipate the great Thanksgiving dinner to be served when we arrive at home, not just for the holidays, but forever and ever.

LIFE APPLICATION

1. Do you help feed the hungry?
2. Do you encourage and teach those who are spiritually malnourished?
3. Are you guilty of picking and choosing Scriptures you want to believe?
4. Do you read some Scriptures over and over for encouragement?
5. Is physical food more important to you than spiritual food?
6. Is there a void in your life that needs to be filled?
7. How are you being spiritually fed?
8. Are you satisfied with where you are and what you are doing at this point in time?
9. Do you ask the Holy Spirit to guide you?
10. Do you spend time each day meditating on the Word of God?

9

I FORGOT WHAT TO REMEMBER

... those looking through the windows grow dim ...
Ecclesiastes 12:3

As the years creep by, memories frequently get lost in the files. One may no longer be able to locate current events in a folder. Information that was once easily accessed may now be irretrievable.

Forgetfulness can't always be blamed on aging. For years, I've had a problem forgetting where I put car keys, mail, and little scraps of paper on which I've written phone numbers or notes. There were many times when my children would stand waiting by the door, ready to leave. One of them would sigh, "We can't go yet—Mom can't find the car keys."

One Sunday the bench where I sat in church jiggled because my muffled laughter shook me inside and out. The preacher had quoted Jesus telling Peter, "I will give unto you the keys of the Kingdom" (Matt. 16:19). I bit my lip. *Lord, I'm so glad you didn't give those keys to me. I'd lose them for sure.* I could envision the blast of the trumpet on that last day and I'd be scurrying around—trying to find the keys to the kingdom.

Often, I go to look for something in the pantry and stand gazing, wondering why I opened the door. Although this is a period of life when we need to be thinking of the hereafter, I don't think it was intended that we should wander from place to place, wondering what we're "here after."

Forgetfulness Can Be Serious

Confusion and the attempt to remember names and events may be a sign of the onset of dementia or Alzheimer's, or it may only be a matter of growing a bit older. While this is a devastating blow for one with this disease, pity the one who must be their caregiver. This attack of the enemy is one of his devious attempts to rob us of our relationships and kill our joy as he relentlessly destroys the mind of someone we love.

Alzheimer's Hits Hard

My brother-in-law is grief-stricken because his beloved wife, Sue, suffers from advanced Alzheimer's. When Charles took us to the nursing home to visit with her, I was shocked. Her mind, once a journal filled with detailed facts, appears to have been coated with acid that has eaten away her memory. Her eyes are now blank. Since the eyes are considered to be the windows of the soul, her soul appears to be gone, leaving her body stranded here.

All Charles has left are beautiful memories of bygone days—of the person Sue used to be. He draws from that well and drinks in the good times, the joy, and the vivaciousness that once flowed from her bright mind. Her ability to recall the past has seemingly dried up inside a shell.

Her ability to think has burned away. Now her brain is like a worthless heap of ashes. I'm afraid if I knock at the door, no one will answer. A whisper tells me, "She doesn't live here anymore."

Charles cares for her body like she was a tiny child. She's even forgotten how to feed herself. He keeps hoping someday a smile will burst across her face, her eyes will light up, and she'll experience a new awakening. For now, this hope eludes him. He's resigned to wait for the time of resurrection, when he will hear God say: "I will repay you for the years the locusts have eaten" (Joel 2:25). Ah, they have so much catching up to do. The time of this awkward type of separation makes the days weary and long. But he's waiting and struggling, anticipating a time when the Lord will restore all that has been lost. Sometimes he prays, "Lord, come quickly."

God's Word assures us He will exchange beauty for ashes, including the worthless residue of a diseased mind. Someday He will give us the ability to view things from His perspective.

> "We don't see things clearly. We're squinting in a fog, peering through a mist. But it won't be long before the weather clears and the sun shines bright! We'll see it all then, see it all as clearly as God sees us, knowing him directly just as he knows us" (1 Cor. 13:12 MSG).

A Remarkable Mystery

An elderly man and his wife both suffered from dementia and lived in a nursing home. One day they heard someone in an adjoining room talking and crying. They inquired and were told it was one of the nurses. "Bring her here," the old man insisted. When the nurse came in, her eyes were tear-stained and she was biting her lip.

"What's wrong, dear?" the old man asked.

The nurse explained, "I've just received a report from my doctor. He's found a large cancerous tumor in my left lung. He is urging me to have surgery immediately."

The elderly couple asked her to come near so they could lay hands on her and pray. After a fervent prayer for healing, the nurse thanked them. When leaving, she assured them, "I'll let you know how the surgery turns out."

In the operating room, the doctors were amazed when they found no trace of the tumor and no sign of cancer. Obviously, God's healing touch was there, even though this old couple's minds were no longer alert.

The nurse confided to their daughter, Jan, weeks later, "I believe

I'd be dead or dying now if your parents hadn't prayed for me. I'm sure they don't even remember praying for me."

When Jan told me this story, her eyes filled with tears of gratitude. "God continued to use Mom and Dad, even when their minds were slipping away."

Some Remain Sweet

Thankfully, some with dementia remain gracious and sweet. Aunt Mary had experienced extremely painful difficulties in life. She was left almost penniless with four small children. Her mother-in-law and sister-in-law had gone to her house soon after her husband's death and stolen everything of value. However, I remembered listening to Aunt Mary sing as she worked. I don't recall hearing her complain. Her contagious laughter bounced off the walls.

As she grew older, dementia began to destroy her memory. One evening, I was driving her home from visiting her daughter. As the evening sun began to set, the sky was ablaze with glorious color. Aunt Mary pointed and exclaimed, "Isn't that a beautiful...picnic?" She chuckled softly. "I can't find my words anymore."

It would be wise for those of us who still have the ability to think, to fill the storehouse of our mind with things that are pure, holy, loving, and joyful (Phil. 4:8). Hopefully, we will maintain and retrieve good basic attitudes, even if our brains aren't functioning as efficiently as they once did.

Some Become Even Sweeter

One mother had never been expressive of love or compliments until after she was diagnosed with Alzheimer's. Her daughter visited one day and her mother greeted her. "Honey, you're so beautiful—and you have beautiful teeth, but you have them in upside down." Some of her statements, like this one, were funny, but they were always kind. Is it possible that attitudes buried deep inside float to the surface when we no longer have control of our thoughts?

Some patients remember old hymns they sang long ago, yet can't remember what happened moments before. We can bless those with memory loss by singing to them—old songs as well as contemporary ones. We have the opportunity to fill their rooms with praise and lift their spirits.

There Comes a Time to Let Our Loved Ones Go

Judith sat with her dying mother who was in advanced stages of Alzheimer's. She hovered close to her bedside, holding her hand, praying for her, asking for the Lord's will to be done. Judith fell asleep and dreamed a spiraling cloud rose over her mom's bed. Her mother was in the midst of that cloud—radiant, youthful, and beautiful—just as she'd looked when she modeled in her youth. Judith was startled that the likeness she saw was similar to magazine pictures she'd seen of her mother in her younger years.

When Judith woke up, she leaned close and said, "Mom, you can go now. I'll be all right, and I'll take care of my brothers." She left the nursing home and drove away. When she arrived home, there was a message on her answering machine. "Your mother passed away soon after you left." Judith was blessed to be able to recall the image of her mother being restored, beautiful, and fluent again.

> "But let me reveal to you a wonderful secret. We will not all die, but we will all be transformed! It will happen in a moment, in the blink of an eye, when the last trumpet is blown. For when the trumpet sounds, those who have died will be raised to live forever" (1 Cor. 15:51–52 NLT).

Reach Out to Caregivers

Most articles written about patients with Alzheimer's are about symptoms and progression of the disease. I pray they discover a way to stop or reverse this horrible assault, but for now, I'm deeply concerned about those who care for them. How difficult it must be, when the child or spouse must finally place the patient in a nursing home. Many struggle with nagging doubts and guilt because they think they could have possibly taken care of their loved one a little while longer. It's alarming to hear that a number of caretakers, determined to continue to take care of their mates, end up dying before their patient.

At best, caregivers experience many emotions such as fear, anger, and frustration. Depression, hopelessness, and self-pity may follow. Their situation is surely more difficult than those of us who've lost a loved one through death.

As compassionate followers of Christ, we need to reach out to these caregivers, although those of us who've never experienced their trauma can't fully empathize with them. A support group is likely to be invaluable to those closest to the patient. The members lean on one another and share their burdens.

My prayer is for those of you who care for a loved one in this condition. I pray our Father will give you wisdom each step of the way and give you the strength to hold steady even when every resource in you is being strained.

Did You Forget Something?

Some say God didn't give older women babies because they'd forget where they put them. That's not only a problem for older women. I didn't do very well with my own children.

When our youngest, Chip, was three, we visited a church an hour's drive from where we lived. Since it was an evening service and it would be late when we arrived home, I dressed the children for bed before we left the church. We made a pallet in the back of the station wagon where they'd fall asleep and we could slip them into their own beds when we arrived home.

After the service, we put them in the car and stood outside to visit with church members. Without our knowledge, Chip slid across and crawled out the opposite door and went back to play. We finished our conversation and drove away without counting little heads.

As we walked into the house, the phone was ringing. It was the preacher from the church we'd visited. "We take care of all lost children."

"W-what?"

"Have you counted your kids? You left one of them in the church yard." I gasped, but before I could say anything, he continued. "But listen, why don't you leave him and come back to the meeting tomorrow night? He can wear some of our kid's clothes tomorrow."

As you can imagine, I was mortified, but Chip was happy to stay there. We were relieved not to have to drive back that night—an extra hundred-mile trip.

When we walked in the building the following evening, the preacher announced, "Here come Joseph and Mary—back to the temple to get their son."

How blessed we are that God doesn't forget His children. "Can a mother forget the infant at her breast, walk away from the baby she bore? But even if mothers forget, I'd never forget you" (Isa. 49:15 MSG).

How Can We Keep Our Minds Healthy?

It is imperative to keep our minds stimulated by crossword puzzles, Sudoku, research, and memorization, though these may not be enough. Challenging thinking and physical exercise are helpful. Some medications and vitamins may stall the progression—somewhat.

Passages of scripture tell us we can have the mind of Christ and that our mind can be renewed. I pray these scriptures regularly. Time will tell if this is a deterrent to memory loss. Beyond that, my hope has been relegated to faith and trust.

Memorizing scripture has proven to strengthen the memory. It has many benefits. It's not only good for our minds—it is good for our souls. When I turned seventy-five, I felt a nudging to memorize Jesus' Sermon on the Mount. The idea kept bouncing around in my mind as if it were an urging from the Lord. I resisted. "I can't remember a sentence—much less three chapters of the Bible." Distractions didn't cause the prompting to go away. Reluctantly, I made note cards with portions of scripture on them. I recorded the sermon to listen to at night as I fell asleep. I copied the recording and kept one in my car to rehearse verses as I drove.

I reviewed the scriptures I'd written on note cards as I waited for doctor's appointments or for the oil to be changed in my car. After three months of memorizing the 111 verses, I was asked to recite them in public on four different occasions.

As an added benefit, I seldom just sat and stared into space, allowing my mind to play tag with every thought darting through my head. By memorizing scripture or other mind-stimulating activities, we can choose to meditate on the best instead of the worst, the beautiful instead of the ugly, things to praise instead of things to curse. We are blessed when we focus on joyful and positive thoughts.

Our God Is a God of Restoration

Even when physical and mental conditions trip us up, we can be assured that as we hold onto God, we're safe in His hands until we cross the finish line. It will be in His timing. Whatever is missing, malfunctioning or broken will be restored and renewed. For right now, however, we can choose to saturate our minds with His Word and grow closer to Him.

We all hope and pray our minds will stay alert as long as we're left here on planet earth. I pray that in every season, we'll do everything in our power to make our lives count for God. He will help us redeem whatever time is left.

Be Enthusiastic

As time slips away, it is easy to lose our enthusiasm. Merriam-Webster gives the definition of the word "enthusiastic" as "showing excitement and eager enjoyment." There's no better reason to experience incredible joy than knowing we're a child of God with Jesus as our older Brother.

Enthusiasm is energizing and usually includes others. When we live above and beyond selfish interests, we can reach out to people and embrace those outside our immediate circle. God's Holy Spirit can give us the animation to brighten the world.

A friend volunteers to go to a food pantry one day a week, to feed the hungry and prepare food baskets to give to the poor. She comes home excited and energized because her actions have made a difference in the lives of others.

Another senior, who felt she had no other talents, goes to the nursery at a local hospital to rock preemie babies. The list of possibilities is endless.

A passion for something enlarges our world. My passion at this point is to reach out with encouragement to those who are growing older—to plant seeds of optimism that will spur older citizens to stand tall and hold steady during difficult times. In that way, their lives will be a living legacy to leave for those who follow.

LIFE APPLICATION

1. Are you concerned about losing your mental capabilities?
2. Do you know of someone who suffers from some form of dementia?
3. How do you keep active physically, mentally, and spiritually?
4. Are you willing to reach out to a caretaker who's been given the responsibility of caring for an Alzheimer's patient?
5. Is there something you can be passionate about?
6. Have you tried memorizing scriptures to develop your mental capabilities?
7. Do you include challenging activities in your schedule?
8. List creative ways to stimulate your mind.
9. Write out scriptures you can memorize about renewing the mind and having the mind of Christ.
10. Are you enthusiastic?

10

NEW DOOR MAY BE OPENING

... when the doors to the street are closed ...
Ecclesiastes 12:4

It's time to stop beating on closed doors and stop looking back. Most doors are permanently locked behind yesterdays. We may not move as fast as we once did, but we can continue to push ahead, looking for doors of opportunity to crack open. "It makes no difference who you are or where you're from—if you want God and are ready to do as he says, the door is open" (Acts 10:35 MSG).

God Sometimes Closes Doors

I don't want to get my hands in the way of any door God may be closing. I was five years old when my sister, "Sis," nineteen years older than I, took the three of us younger children and her mother-in-law to the circus.

When we started to drive home, I stood behind the older lady in the front seat of the car with my hand wrapped around the post between the front and back door. Before I moved my hand, she slammed the door on my fingers, then opened it and shut it again! In spite of my pain, I was too timid to cry out.

Sis turned around and saw tears streaming down my cheeks and scolded. "Why are you crying? I took you to the circus."

I wailed. "My fingers are in the door."

Both women in the front seat were mortified. I learned from that accident not to stick my hand in a door when God is ready to close it.

Some Aren't Listening to God

A visiting preacher spoke at church, begging for us to help his congregation save the retirement home they operated. Adequate funds were no longer available to keep the doors open, and resources from their church members had dried up. The board encouraged the congregation to mortgage their homes in order to keep the facility in operation. This didn't seem right. I approached the pastor after he spoke and asked, "Is it possible that God is trying to tell you it's time to close the doors?" He looked astounded. "We've never thought about that. Perhaps we do need to make sure this is God's plan, rather than our own."

Doors That Close

Age sneaked up on my blind side and doors began to close as my health and energy began to fade. For fifteen years, the management of Hidden Manna Christian Retreat Center had been a wonderful experience. However, I decided I shouldn't wait much longer, as age and health might begin to hamper my ability to cook, clean, and mow. I loved my job and the ministry, but no doubt it was time to slow down.

I told the board when I reached my seventy-fifth birthday, it would probably be a good idea to step back. They agreed. God turned my attention to things I *could* continue, such as speaking, seminars, teaching, mentoring, and writing. While I knew there were risks in transplanting an old, established tree, it would be necessary for me to be transplanted to another spot. But I trusted I could still bear fruit in another garden. I packed up my personal belongings and moved.

When we've passed the prime of our lives, Satan would have us believe we can no longer be productive. Perhaps if we listen closely, however, we'll hear God calling us in a different direction. God can still use us as a nurturer, to give water in the form of encouragement to those who are weary. Our Heavenly Father calls for workers to go out and bring in ripened souls ready to be harvested.

Doors are open in the kingdom for God's older citizens as well as the young. I see light seeping under a new door that's beginning to crack open. In my neighborhood I can minister and teach Bible classes. The Holy Spirit is there to guide us in reaching out in large and small ways—even stuffing envelopes at the church office or taking cookies across the street. Even small acts of kindness are noticed by God.

God may not open doors that are large or impressive. Some opportunities may come in the form of driving someone to the grocery store or doctor's office. We can look for resources to find where people can get the help they need—whether it is for counsel, food, or money. An opening door is our cue that we're to continue to move ahead. We find fulfillment when we're in the center of God's will.

Watch for New Doors to Open

Retirement is a time when we've left the workplace where people sometimes kicked doors open by force. Manipulative people picked the locks to get what they wanted. Those bent on self-serving ambitions often push, shove, and even step on others to be sure they get through doors they want or think they are entitled to.

When some retire, they feel unneeded and possibly unwanted. Their goals and incentives shrink because they believe their life counts for very little now. Discouragement may cause their immune system to falter. Depression and apathy may make them vulnerable to various health issues.

Knowing God has a purpose for us fills us with hope. He opens new doors with our mustard seed faith and offers vistas greater than we ever dreamed. It is beautiful to watch a bit of faith open a door no man can close. Doors with hinges of faith are oiled by the Holy Spirit. This causes them to swing wide open. This is more effective than WD-40.

On a trip to China as a tourist, I had the opportunity to teach a class in an underground Bible school. Students came from all over the country to prepare to be pastors, teachers, and missionaries.

The following year, I began to think of possibly returning to teach for a longer period of time. I tried to dismiss the idea since I'd not had training to do this type of work. I didn't speak the language, and it would involve teaching, using an interpreter, a full six hours a day for a week.

An outreach like this would be challenging and a little scary—especially since I was in my mid-seventies, but the thought kept recycling in my mind. Finally, I mentioned it to a friend.

She called me the following day and said, "If you decide to go, my husband and I have enough frequent flyer mileage to send you." I was flabbergasted, but decided I should at least check to see if the school needed me. I emailed the director of the mission and sent him a brief resume. He sent me a return email the following day, stating: "We're inviting you to participate in what we believe is one of the most exciting outreaches in the Christian world today." My heart leapt. *I'd heard from God.*

A lady at church found out about my plans and asked me how much money I needed. I told her, "My airfare is taken care of, but the director said I needed a minimum of $750 to take care of all other expenses." She pulled out her checkbook and wrote me a check for a thousand dollars. She said, "I don't want you to be out a dime of your own money."

My niece called me before my second trip the next year and sent me a check for twenty-five hundred dollars to cover my entire trip. When time for the third trip rolled around, people would randomly walk up to me and hand me money—enough to provide for everything I needed. For my fourth trip, the church sponsored a BBQ and paid for my entire trip, as well as for someone to go with me.

God had not only opened the door but ushered me through it. While there, I taught the Bible and prayed for students. When I shared my own struggles, victories, and defeats, it encouraged them to hold steady in their walk with the Lord.

A Soldier for God

When we enlist in God's army, the enemy awaits inside these new doors. He sneaks up as a sniper, brandishing weapons of fear and doubt. His demons threaten, hoping we'll scramble back into foxholes or the safety of our homes. But God's Holy Spirit gives us a boldness to go with Him—no turning back.

Several asked me, "Aren't you afraid to go to a country that is so opposed to Christianity?" I chuckled. "If God commissions me to go, I'm afraid *not* to go."

Preparing for the Inevitable Door

Carey had been in the hospital for a week. When the doctor told us there was nothing else they could do, he asked the children and me if they should keep him on life support. I said, "I think he's able to understand you. Talk to him." We gathered around his bed in intensive care as the doctor explained his prognosis. Carey didn't hesitate. He made motions, indicating he wanted the doctor to pull the plugs. The staff did as he directed, and Carey was moved to a private room. There, with labored speech, Carey made a recording to be played to the church at his funeral. He urged believers to praise God more freely in worship.

As visitors came for a last visit, he asked them to talk about happy times, to read scriptures, and sing to him. He was surrounded with singing, prayers, and acts of love. Some held his hands; others rubbed his feet or washed his face with a cool cloth. Most prayed for God's will to be done.

The night Carey died, Chip was alone with him in the room. He prayed, "Lord, either heal him or take him home." Within minutes, Carey stopped breathing. Chip rushed to the nurse's desk and shouted, "Call the doctor!" He ran into the waiting room nearby, where I was talking with friends and urged me, "Come quickly!" I rushed to

Carey's room and stood on one side of his bed while the doctor stood on the other, checking his pulse. In a few moments, she spoke softly, "He's gone."

Tears streamed down my cheeks as I looked up and whispered, "Lord Jesus, receive his spirit." And then I turned, stomped my foot and spoke sternly, "Satan, you did *not* win; you may have closed one door, but God will open others."

The statement about God opening other doors became a self-fulfilling prophesy. After a period of grieving, God began to work in many different ways in my life. I was grateful God's people had been taught to care for the widows and orphans. I was surrounded by wonderful Christians who helped me get though those following dark days.

Over the last thirty years since my husband's death, I've had many opportunities to teach, speak, write, and minister to others by helping them build on a solid foundation of faith. Before, most of my Christian activities involved working with Carey on seminars, retreats, home Bible studies, and entertaining. After he was gone, the transition came slowly. First, I took in an unwed mother to stay with me until her baby was born and adopted. I developed other gifts that had lain dormant. I discovered new ways to make a difference in people's lives.

I obtained a key to the church building and started going there early each morning to pray. One morning, when I woke up, I remembered my daughter-in-law had borrowed the church key. I was tempted to roll over and go back to sleep, but felt a strong prodding to get up. As I dressed and drove to church, I mumbled. "This is useless. All the doors are locked."

When I drove in the parking lot, another woman from church drove up beside me. I was surprised because no one had ever joined me before. I explained I didn't have a key, but we went ahead and checked the doors. One *was* open! We went in for an hour of prayer and were both blessed. Neither of us questioned who arranged for a door to be unlocked.

There Are Many Things to Do

When Marie Banister visited a child in MD Anderson Cancer Center years ago, she took a pretty, soft pillow. When she saw how other children wanted to touch and feel it, she enlisted other women. Over the years, they made and gave away over 120,000 pillows to children in the hospital. She continued this ministry until her death at age eighty-nine. We must not underestimate the value of a small idea to reach out to comfort or help others.

My friend Joanne, in her mid-seventies, started going to a juvenile justice facility to teach Bible lessons and pray with delinquent teenage girls. She encouraged them to believe they can still have a good life, regardless of how they have messed up their lives. Emails and letters from those who have returned home tell her they are making good choices and starting over again.

My brother-in-law, Jim, who at this writing is in his eighties, has made it his ministry to do odd jobs for widows and single mothers in his community. His outreach is loved and appreciated by many of us. I asked him, "Don't you get tired of doing difficult and dirty jobs?" He grinned and said, "No, not really. It gives me pleasure to know I'm offering a service for those who can't do these things for themselves." He's proof that things we do for ourselves give us temporary satisfaction, but the things we do for others leave us with a warm afterglow. He has a true servant's heart. At church, they call him a sheep dog—one who looks after the sheep.

If you've not been involved in reaching out, begin by taking baby steps. As God sees our willingness to serve, He opens more and bigger doors of opportunity. Abraham Lincoln expressed great wisdom: "I will prepare and someday my chance will come."

Choose the Best

We're tempted to pamper ourselves by doing only what we want—playing golf, watching TV, going out to eat, or shopping. The bumper sticker "Shop 'til you drop" seems pointless. It can be a blessing or a curse that we're allowed to choose what we want to do with our lives. If we're wise, we'll ask God to show us what He has planned, rather than being left to pick and choose what we want to do with our time and money.

When I moved into the community where I live, a neighbor asked, "Do you play golf or tennis?"

"No, I don't.

"Do you play bridge?"

I shook my head. "Sorry."

When I mentioned this to my daughter-in-law, Teri said, "Did you tell her you have a life?" Please don't misunderstand me. There is absolutely nothing wrong with any of these activities. But the time spent with things that are only for our own pleasure can easily become the focal point of our lives.

Since most seniors are no longer employed, there's a temptation to get involved in mindless talk and gossip. Texting and chitchatting on the phone have the potential of being traps to say more than we should. Some become so absorbed in Facebook and other social networking sites, they spend the bulk of their time sending messages about almost every move they make.

"Set a guard over my mouth, LORD; keep watch over the door of my lips" (Ps. 141:3).

If we're willing to follow, God can lead us to unparalleled heights.

> "By entering through faith into what God has always wanted to do for us—set us right with him, make us fit for him—we have it all together with God because of our Master Jesus. And that's not all: We throw open our doors to God and discover at the same moment that he has already thrown open his door to us" (Rom. 5:1–2 MSG).

We are free to choose which doors of opportunity we will open and go through.

The Power of Encouragement

When I was being introduced at a retreat, the lady told the audience. "Louise probably saved my life many years ago. She counseled me about some emotional problems I wrestled with." I was embarrassed, but I couldn't remember ever meeting the lady. It's incredible how a little encouragement can make such an impact. It's sobering to think that a casual conversation could change the course of someone's life.

Senior citizens may well be Christianity's greatest untapped resource for doing good. Are some things stirring in your mind, yet? Why not be a conduit for God's light to shine through? Many seniors need no financial support, and they can offer years of invaluable experience.

LIFE APPLICATION

1. Have you had a door of opportunity close on you recently?
2. As you grow older, are you looking for new or different things you can do?
3. What talents or gifts would you like to develop in the future?
4. Name factors you may need to consider when pursuing a new goal.
5. Do you think you're too old to change your habits?
6. Are you watching your diet and exercising to keep yourself in good health?
7. Are you focused too much on yourself and your own whims?
8. Are there negative thoughts that Satan has put in your mind about aging?
9. Are there habits you need to break to keep from being stuck in a rut?
10. Do you have the courage to step out and volunteer in ways to help others?

11

THE DAILY GRIND SHUTS DOWN

… the sound of grinding fades …
Ecclesiastes 12:4

I found my significance and self-worth in my work as a diagnostician. It left an empty spot in my life when I retired from my job. The feelings of responsibility seemed to have slipped through a hole in my pocket and left nothing to fill that need.

I cleaned out my desk at the office and sat at the head table for a retirement party. It was then I discovered they were no longer giving gold watches at retirement. Likely, they figured time wouldn't be important to me, since I'd no longer be punching a time clock.

My meager retirement benefits caused me to hit the ground—not running, but with a dull thud. There'd be no golden parachute to float leisurely through fluffy clouds for the remainder of my days.

Father Time led me out and quietly closed the door to the sounds of the workplace. The daily grind came to a halt. Along with others, I seemed to feel this past era of employment was the most significant time of life. Everything from then on should be a downhill slide—right? *Wrong.*

The workaholic demon darted about my brain, relentlessly whispering, "Retirement implies you're nigh on to useless now." Frustration and self-pity reinforced this accusation.

Animosity knocked at the door, ready to join these fellow tormentors. I had to decide whether I'd offer him a nice warm place to build his nest and hatch his eggs, or kick him out the door and tell him to go somewhere else to roost. Thankfully, I chose the latter.

Wait—There's Far More!

The grind of the workplace involved polishing job skills and sanding off rough edges of productivity. My boss often used threats and a hammer and chisel to hack away on poor performance. The emphasis was to do more, better, and faster!

However, if we shift our thoughts and hearts to what the Lord has planned, we'll find God at work on the inside to make our lives more about *who we are* rather than *what we do*. Our Heavenly Father focuses on us as "human beings" rather than "human doings." He's ready to grind off the rough edges of the *outer* man for a whole new purpose and direction for our *inner* man at this stage of the game.

The process God uses to shape us is not unlike that of a sculptor. When we allow God to shape us into a work of art, he takes potentially good raw material and begins to chip away everything that doesn't enhance the art form He envisions. Ungodly chunks of pride are whacked off. He chisels selfishness to shape us into the likeness of His Son. Ouch!

It takes time, some of which is painful, but the Lord is tenacious and patient in His attempt to create a masterpiece. We can refuse to become a work of art—but if we resist God's plan, we'll never have the privilege of being touched by the Master's hand.

Our stubborn wills are like rock. We have to give permission to the One who shapes our future to grind off our resistant attitudes. We may be tempted to pull away from God and hang on to our hardhearted ways. But hopefully, we'll reconsider and yield to His touch, allowing Him to sand off bad traits, letting them fall like sand from our lives.

A Changed Life

My son, Chip, had a rebellious streak as a teen. To say his lifestyle was unacceptable is an understatement. Once, he disappeared for three months before coming back into our lives. I prayed for him for a number of years, seemingly to no avail. I kept pleading, "I want to turn Chip over to You, Lord, but please don't hurt him." Finally, in desperation, I prayed aloud, "God, regardless of what You need to do, either bring someone or something into his life that will cause him to turn his life around."

A couple of weeks later, Chip called with an incredible story. "My friend and I went camping at Lake Dallas. A couple of bums came up with knives and robbed us. Every penny I had to my name was in my wallet. As soon as they left, my buddy suggested we jump in my van to try to get close enough to get their license number. In the chase, we skidded around a corner on a gravel road and rolled the van. I crashed through the windshield into the pathway of an oncoming car."

I covered my mouth in horror as I listened to his story. In the back of my mind I was thinking, *This is one time I'm glad he was hard headed!*

Chip continued. "A car came barreling down on me. In a dazed state, I raised my hand to plead, 'God don't let them hit me.' The car screeched to a stop and the people called an ambulance to take me to the hospital where they stitched me up. I'm okay and at my brother Rick's house."

I sensed a softness in his voice as he asked, "Mom, could you come get me?"

Carey and I drove to Dallas to bring him home. After we picked him up, we went by the police impound lot to check on his van. It was crushed like a Styrofoam cup, not worth the price to bail it out. We drove back to Houston in awkward silence.

The following Sunday, Chip went to church with us. I overheard him telling some of his friends. "God knew what He had to do to get my attention." Indeed, the Lord had used a drastic measure in an attempt to chop off a chunk of his rebellious spirit.

This incident jump-started a 180-degree turnaround in his life. He not only recommitted his life to the Lord, but went farther, to make God his number one priority. Now, years later, he is sold out to God, and he and his wife are pastors of a church. The Lord is now number one in his life.

As a loving father, Chip is a true family man. He beams with pride over his precious wife and children. He likes to brag. "I always dreamed of being surrounded by beautiful women, but never dreamed the reality would come in the form of my wife and three beautiful daughters."

When the Lord allowed an explosion in his life, it was painful. But I'm convinced the Father wouldn't have used dynamite if a firecracker would have done the job.

Thank You, Lord. You are a wise and dynamic force, intent on your children becoming the ones you created them to be. In order for this to happen, we must be willing for Him to do whatever it takes to get us and our loved ones to turn to Him.

Iron Sharpens Iron

Often God allows someone to be in close proximity that grinds on our nerves. God brought such a person to live with me. Her personality caused many of my negative traits to rise to the surface. We clashed. She was serious, while I was flippant. By nature, she was super-organized—I was not.

Both of us loved the Lord, so we should have gotten along great, right? Wrong. She took it upon herself to *help* me. Buzzing around in the kitchen with my "type A" personality, she cautioned me: "Use a pot holder to lift that skillet, it's hot. Did you wash the pinto beans before you put them on to cook? Watch out for that open cabinet door and don't bump your head." I stuffed my irritation and gritted my teeth as her cautions continued to grind on my nerves.

In her attempts to help, I felt controlled and manipulated.

Agitation kindled a fire within, until one day, I lashed out. "I don't need you as a mother, standing over me to monitor everything I do. Thank you very much. I'm past sixty-five and I've managed quite well for decades before you ever came into my life." She retaliated by writing me a scathing letter, listing the grievances she had against me.

In retrospect, there'd been too little application of biblical principles in my life. I read the Word daily, but if you'd asked me what I read about, I might have answered, "About fifteen minutes."

> "You have your heads in your Bibles constantly because you think you'll find eternal life there. But you miss the forest for the trees. These scriptures are all about me! And here I am, standing right before you, and you aren't willing to receive from me the life you say you want" (John 5:39–40 MSG).

I seriously considered suggesting this lady and I go our separate ways. But then, we decided to start each day by reading brief passages of scripture together and journaling about what we thought the Lord would say to us that day. God didn't hesitate to point out a number of flaws in each of us. Every morning, we shared our thoughts and prayed together.

This simple routine began to evoke a change in our relationship. In the past, our lives had been a tiny flicker of light rather than a beacon on a hill. But God's beam of light revealed our rough edges. We prayed for Him to chisel off bad attitudes and polish our rough spots. We actually welcomed this grinding. He loved us too much to leave us as we were. As time passed, the sound of this grinding began to fade.

This common practice evolved into a long-lasting friendship in which the two of us reached out to minister to others. Our differences were not only minimized, but each of our strengths covered the other's weaknesses. The heavy tenseness lifted. We set boundaries and worked out a division of chores. Our interactions began to run smooth, and we became the very best of friends.

We included guests in our daily devotionals, and as they observed how we worked through our difficulties, they felt free to talk about their own interpersonal struggles. As we shared and applied God's Word, He did a refining work in us.

It was a beautiful experience—when we decided to let God polish us *up* before He polished us *off*.

Spread Your Love

A friend suggested, "Look past your surroundings here and reach out to others. You'll please God by pleasing others." We were serious about our lives becoming more meaningful and decided to look for opportunities surrounding us. It was a blessing to know we were needed.

We asked our Father to clarify and use any spiritual gifts that had lain dormant. In our heart of hearts, we knew it wasn't too late for God to use us in meaningful ways.

I determined to look beyond the barbecue grill in the back yard and past the flat screen television in the living room. There were many places we could volunteer. We spent time in prayer rooms, going on mission trips, and taking food to the sick. We zeroed in on things we could make right in the world, rather than focus on the things that were wrong in our immediate surroundings.

Shine Still Brighter

Ah yes, we took time to read His Word more. We became better acquainted with the Bible and praised our Heavenly Father's holy name. In Revelation a Scripture captured our attention. It speaks of those who stand before God throughout eternity, repeating, "Holy, Holy, Holy, Lord God Almighty,' who was and is and is to come" (Rev. 4:8).

We thought of this concept as a giant disco ball. Each time we looked up to praise the Lord, we discovered a new and magnificent virtue of God's greatness. Facet after shining facet reflected His glory

91

and majesty. We could marvel over Jehovah God forever, without growing weary or seemingly repetitious. This glorious incentive encouraged us to spend more time praising the Lord for His innumerable attributes.

The Rest of Our Years Can Be the Best of Our Years

It's strange that God sometimes waits until the evening shadows of life begin to fade before fulfilling His greatest purposes though his children. God sent Abraham back to square one during his old age. He chose him to begin populating the world when he was almost a hundred years old. I'd like to say, *Lord, choose me," but I don't want to be like Sarah and have a baby at this stage of the game. Shiver me timbers!*

God literally put Moses "out to pasture" for forty years before calling him to his greatest assignment of setting the Israelites free. Some say the apostle Paul was not ready to be used by God until he became a "basket case" when lowered over the wall in a basket and remained out of sight for a few years. No doubt, during this time, the Lord was grinding off some of his rough edges before sending him out as a polished missionary.

A remarkable number of people make their greatest contribution late in life. Mary Frances, an older woman at church, retired after teaching at a local university. She busied herself in the community and became involved in a number of outreaches. She volunteered to work with benevolent causes and staffed the prayer room. She commented in the midst of all her involvement, "I just wish I could do more."

The doctors discovered Mary Frances had cancer, but she kept going until she had to be hospitalized. When the preacher visited her, she demanded, "You have to get me out of here. I have too much to do." She died the following day at age eighty-nine. I suppose God thought she was talking to Him, so He obliged her—and *got her out of there.*

Most of the people in the city knew her. She had touched many lives. She was elected Woman of the Year shortly before her death. Her determination to go out and help others never came to a grinding halt. *Lord, give us the commitment to live a full life until the time when You're ready to call us home.*

A Time for Complete Submission

After the sound of the grinding of our jobs has "grown low," it's time to step down and ask God to continue to sand and polish us.

> "Calling the crowd to join his disciples, he said, 'Anyone who intends to come with me has to let me lead. You're not in the driver's seat; I am" (Mark 8:34 MSG).

When we yield to God's deliberate touch, we can ask Him to work on each aspect of our lives until an exquisite sculpture is complete. It requires dedication and perseverance to yield to God's masterful touch.

> "We pray that you'll have the strength to stick it out over the long haul—not the grim strength of gritting your teeth but the glory-strength God gives. It is the strength that endures the unendurable and spills over into joy, thanking the Father who makes us strong enough to take part in everything bright and beautiful that he has for us" (Col. 1:11–12 MSG).

Be Creative

Creativity can be a polished gift that makes us shine. The Lord gave us that gift to help us come up with great, new ideas. A church invited me to speak at their weekend retreat for a group of about 250 women. In preparing my materials, I kept thinking of skits that would illustrate the lessons I planned to teach. Though I was in my sixties, I'd never acted before. It was a stretch to use my creativity.

The first night, I was dressed in costume. Right before going onstage, I panicked. *Oh dear, there're probably a number of actresses in the audience and quite possibly some who even teach drama.* I trembled, my heart pounded, and my mouth went dry. Suddenly, deep within, the Lord whispered, "If you're afraid, it's because you don't think I have given you the talent to do this, you missed My leading, or you want to impress the audience. None of these excuses are acceptable."

I swallowed hard. *Forgive me, Lord. I'm ready—front and center.* All of a sudden, it didn't matter if the people thought I was good or not. I would be obedient to what God led me to do in spite of my amateurish performance. As a result, God used the skits powerfully to change lives—including mine.

Likely, we all have creativity pushed to a back shelf of our minds—asleep for years—waiting to be awakened. Come on, Grandma Moses. If you love art, invite that talent to come forth. God's gift of creativity takes many forms: knitting, playing an instrument, or taking up a new hobby—anything that enlists our God-given talents. You might find sign language a creative way of expressing your heart by signing and singing. Scratch your head—see if there's something itching to come out. Better still, ask God for suggestions.

The Master's work of chiseling and grinding, sandpapering and polishing, is a part of the transformation process. We can refuse to get bogged down in the daily grind of living by asking God, "Sand off my rough edges and help me to be more creative."

Are We Diamonds in the Rough?

Stories are told about finding and cutting the Hope Diamond. The most skilled diamond cutter in the world was commissioned for the task. He was entrusted with the rough diamond and kept it for a year—looking at it, touching it, turning it over and over to discover the best way to enhance its exquisite beauty and size. He used his meticulous skill in cutting this magnificent stone.

I'd like to think God is watching us, waiting until He's sure we're ready to hold still on His work table. There, He'll smooth off the rough edges so we can become a work of art of great value to Him and others.

No doubt our Heavenly Father has been chipping on our rough edges for years. Perhaps He's ground off most of the coarse places and is ready to start polishing on us as jewels, to complete the final touches.

> "The Lord their God will save his people in that day, as a
> Shepherd caring for his sheep. They shall shine in his
> land as glittering jewels in a crown. How wonderful and
> beautiful all shall be!" (Zech. 9:16–17 TLB).

So here we are—diamonds in the rough. God would have us sparkle so that the reflection of Jesus will be seen from every angle, every facet. He places us where we'll catch the light of the Son. "I made you grow like a plant in the field. You grew up and became tall and became like a beautiful jewel" (Ezek. 16:7 NCV). Someday, I want to end up in God's jewelry box.

It's time to pray for a faith that will deepen our relationship with God, reflecting a sparkling and abundant life. Let me invite you along with Robert Browning, "Grow old along with me! The best is yet to be."

LIFE APPLICATION

1. What can you do to keep retirement from making you feel unimportant?
2. Do you have conflicting feelings about leaving the workplace?
3. Is God working on any rough edges in your life?
4. Do you trust God enough to turn over your loved ones to His care?
5. Do you read the Bible and journal as you write about the struggles you face?
6. Who do you know who has remained active as they grew older?
7. Make a list of those who may be watching how you live your life. (And there are *others* you are not aware of.)
8. What excuses do you make that keep you from doing something new or different?
9. Are there areas of creativity you could develop?
10. How might you, at your age, be a blessing and of great value to those around you?

12

BE GOD'S AMBASSADOR OF JOY

... when men rise up at the sound of birds ...
Ecclesiastes 12:4

One of the benefits of retirement is I no longer need a jangling alarm to wake me up to go to work. My job no longer calls my name. So, what happened when I settled into this new routine? My eyes pop open at the loud crack of dawn. And twist and turn as I might, I can't go back to sleep. I unwittingly become an early bird. So much for the fact that I don't care much for worms! A saying I remember from childhood makes me chuckle: "Tis spring and the birdies peep; I wish they'd shut up and let me sleep."

However, rather than chirping birds being an irritant, I like to think of them as a wake-up call singing, "Welcome to my world." Perhaps in bird language they're announcing, "This is the day which the LORD hath made, we will rejoice and be glad in it" (Ps. 118:24 KJV). Listen carefully; one bird seems to be singing, "Cheer-ee, Cheer-ee, Cheer-ee."

The mood we wake up with often sets the tone for the day. That well-worn expression about people getting up on the wrong side of the bed contains an element of truth. But thankfully, we have a choice as to how we hit the floor in the morning. We're encouraged to take control of our thoughts, so our minds don't flip back to yesterday's struggles or skip ahead to today's or tomorrow's concerns. Each morning we should ask God for His guidance and the way He wants to orchestrate the plans He has for us—each day.

The chirping of birds and their flight through the air can lift our spirits from early morning until we hit the pillow at night.

> "So you'll go out in joy, you'll be led into a whole and complete life. The mountains and the hills will lead the parade, bursting with song. All the trees of the forest will lead the procession, exuberant with applause" (Isa. 55:12 MSG).

Taking a walk early in the morning gives us an opportunity to soak up the beauty and blessings of the great outdoors. There is an element of peace in nature, so breathe in this gift and breathe out the cares of the world.

Even before God formed man, I believe He sprinkled joy, like dew, throughout the universe. Perhaps He sat back with deep satisfaction and listened to everything He created sing and clap their hands. "Let the fields be jubilant, and everything in them. Then all the trees of the forest will sing for joy" (Ps. 96:12). Though we may not be able to audibly hear these beautiful responses, thoughts of them strike a pleasant cord in our hearts.

Imagine the earth, infused with joy, bowing before the throne of God. The heavens, blanketed with stars, sing praises to God—while angels shout their loudest praise. The whole earth must resonate with laughter, bursting forth in song. "What supports the foundation? Who placed the cornerstone, while morning stars sang, and angels rejoiced?" (Job 38:6–7 CEV).

When God spoke each element into existence, I imagine it must have responded by glorifying the Creator of the Universe for His masterful craftsmanship. We too, rejoice in Him. "On your feet now—applaud GOD! Bring a gift of laughter, sing yourselves into his presence" (Ps. 100:1–2 MSG).

Look at nature and experience God's waterfall of love. Love and joy sent to be the constant companions of believers. We lift our hands to accept all the gifts our Father showers on His children. Rivers of grace and mercy cascade down from the hills and inspire us to sing along with nature.

Though we may not hear well, we can be confident God always hears us. Praise seems to be the easiest way to enter into God's presence. It sets the stage for Him to draw near to His children.

Peace and joy reign in our hearts when we're convinced He's perfectly capable of handling everything that happens in life. The One who numbers each hair of the tangled mess on our head also knows how to help us comb through every tiny detail of our messy lives.

The sparrows and swallows pick incredible places to build their nests. "Even the sparrow has found a home, and the swallow a nest for herself ... a place near your altar, LORD Almighty, my King and my God" (Ps. 84:3). We can follow the example of these birds by nesting peacefully in the presence of Almighty God.

Ambassadors of Joy

I believe birds are God's ambassadors of joy. Their warbles are instruments of praise. Because of our name, some refer to us as "Looney birds." My son, Paul, is a psychiatrist and is teased about his name—a shrink named Looney! My younger son, Chip, owns a couple of music stores, so you can imagine what kind of tunes he's likely to play. With a name like ours, we're committed to join the rest of the songbirds in a chorus of praise. I find the name Looney appropriate for the Looney Tidbits—the videos filled with chuckles I post on social media.

The morning Paul sent his son off to kindergarten, he explained to him. "Others will probably make fun of you because our last name is Looney, and that word means crazy." Adam was disturbed to hear this and was somewhat hesitant about going to school. However, he came home several days later all smiles and announced, "I know why our name is 'Looney.' It's because we're crazy about each other."

My mother's name was Byrd, and we found her to be a cherry

spot in our day—bringing peace and laughter into our home. She too, as a Byrd, was an ambassador of joy.

Falling Asleep at the Wrong Times

As people grow older, they often wake up with the birds, but they also "go to bed with the chickens." We tend to fall asleep at inappropriate times. Some of us drop off during the nightly ten o'clock news—missing the weather report we stayed up to hear.

Perhaps we'll catch bits and pieces of the news of the world's problems which will give us input to tell others how to solve the world's problems!

Sometimes I'll be watching a movie and fall asleep and miss the ending. That's frustrating. Oh well, I might as well stretch and engage in a long, noisy yawn, brush my teeth, and go to bed. In a couple of days, I won't remember ever seeing the movie!

Let Joy Be Like a Birdsong in Our Hearts

Joy helps us stay young. What a blessing it would be to have peace and joy as our companions while traveling this last journey. Life would not only be enhanced, but good attitudes would also flourish in the presence of these two friends.

Praise and joy swing the gates open that lead into the presence of God. Joy makes the route to eternity much easier. Our steps are energized and burdens become lighter when joy skips alongside. Birds chirp and sing as they build their nests. We would do well to sing as we nestle close to God to rest.

In order to make room for joy, we must sweep out complaining and pessimism, lest dirt gets tracked in and spreads over our outlook. We come into the Throne Room to receive our booster shot of joy for the day. How rewarding to know God's presence builds our immune system against grumpiness.

Joy is a fruit of the Holy Spirit. It is a small word with great meaning. As children, we were taught the word *joy* stood for **Jesus** first, **O**thers second, and **Y**ourself last. This is possibly the shortest route to experience happiness at the core of our being.

My husband, a psychologist, conducted many seminars. When he spoke, he often used me as the brunt of his jokes. He had one favorite: "Someone asked me if I woke up grumpy every day, and I told them, 'No, sometimes I let her sleep late.'"

After a lecture, a woman approached me. "How can you stand hearing him talk about you the way he does?"

I chuckled. "If I laugh louder than anyone else, everyone will think he's teasing and believe the things he says about me are not really true."

Surrounded by God's Beauty

In order to wake up to the sound of a bird, we can pick one we want to be like. The blue bird is delightful. Some refer to it as the blue bird of happiness. Watching them sail through the air brings me pleasure. We invite them to sit on our shoulder and accompany us throughout the day.

It is encouraging to see the first robin after a long, hard winter. That bird announces that the hope of spring is on its way. We love to be around people who remind us that God is on His way—with good things planned for this new season of our lives. We're grateful for those who encourage us to look beyond present circumstances, when our burdens will be lifted after a long, hard winter of trials. If we approach God with our requests, sandwiched between praise, might He not be pleased to answer those prayers?

A Bird as a Symbol of Peace

It is amazing that God used a dove, a symbol of peace, to deliver an awesome message to Jesus.

> "Just as Jesus was coming up out of the water, he saw
> heaven being torn open and the Spirit descending on him
> like a dove. And a voice came from heaven: 'You are

my Son, whom I love; with you I am well pleased'"
(Mark 1:10–11).

Throughout the world the dove is symbolic of peace. This concept possibly originated when Noah sent a dove from the ark. The first time he released it, the dove flew back to the ark, but the second time it returned with an olive branch in its beak, indicating it was safe to leave the ark and return to solid ground. God chose this wondrous way to bring this welcome message.

The sound of a dove is one of the most soothing of bird songs. Their mellow cooing is relaxing and reassures us, "All is right with the world." Even as we grow older and we don't hear well, we rehearse the memory of the comforting sound of the dove in our minds.

Even more comforting is Jesus' promises of peace. "I am leaving you with a gift—peace of mind and heart. And the peace I give is a gift the world cannot give. So don't be troubled or afraid" (John 14:27 NLT). My prayer is that we will wake up each morning with a quiet peace that passes understanding.

During the early throes of cancer, my husband came out of a store to find a dove perched on the hood of his car. He reached out and the dove hopped in his hand for a brief moment. Though Carey did not receive his healing in this life, the dove appeared as a special silent emissary to assure him of God's presence throughout the challenging months ahead.

Find Time to Spend Alone with God

It can be good for us to "wake up to the sound of the birds"—to read, journal, and pray. This is a time when we're less likely to be interrupted by visitors or phone calls. Jesus set the example by rising early in the morning to go to a quiet place to pray. If that fulfilled one of His needs, then it is much more important for us to rise early to meet with God.

Each person should find his or her own best time to spend alone with the Lord. Since the enemy will attempt to interrupt this special communion with God, it is wise to make the decision that we'll not be distracted by anything less than an earthquake. The rewards are great. "I love them that love me; and those that seek me early shall find me" (Prov. 8:17 KJV).

Plan for a quiet time and place to pray. We're told the mother of Charles and John Wesley spent time with the Lord daily. When she threw her apron over her head, all her ten surviving children knew they were to be quiet and she was not to be bothered. Her apron became her prayer closet. It was a way for her to symbolically close out the sounds surrounding her and speak to her Heavenly Father and listen for His voice.

We should never let the bird's message of joy grow faint. Each morning, we face a new day. We can choose to welcome the morning like the birds. And what better way to stay young at heart than to be God's ambassadors of joy?

LIFE APPLICATION

1. When you can't sleep, what meaningful things can you do?
2. How long has it been since you went outside and listened to the birds and sounds of nature?
3. Do you make a conscious effort to stay in a good mood throughout the day?
4. Have you ever smothered joy by grumbling and complaining?
5. Do you believe God intended for our lives to be joyful?
6. Can joy help you stay healthy emotionally and physically?
7. Do you take time to praise God for His wondrous creation?
8. Are you pleasant to the point that people enjoy being around you?
9. Name various birds and attributes you'd like to mimic.
10. Do you have a special time to spend listening to God?

13

SPEAK UP! I CAN'T HEAR YOU

... but all their songs grow faint ...
Ecclesiastes 12:4

Songs growing faint could be a metaphor of age-related hearing loss. Inability to hear causes us to miss many of the joys in life—the giggles of children, whispers of love, or pertinent lines in movies. I am thankful I have hearing aids.

Hearing Loss

My sister, Ruth, got hearing aids after she discovered she was missing some of the things her grandchildren were saying. After she got hearing aids, she told her husband, "You know, Jim, you aren't mumbling as much as you did."

Jim smiled. "True. And I'm not forced to talk half as much as I did."

I don't quite understand why older people's ears and noses keep growing as they age. Perhaps ears flapping farther outside one's head might capture sound waves and help people hear better. But surely big noses aren't an indication that some of us need to smell better. And I hope it isn't because we've been telling lies or have been too nosey.

Even though I have those wonderful little gadgets called hearing aids, I still miss some things people say, but by watching people, I've learned to read lips a little bit and facial expressions make it easier to get the gist of what people are talking about.

One of my widowed friends came up with a delightful side benefit of getting hearing aids after her hearing loss. Her children thought she was young and attractive enough to find another good man. She wasn't interested. But her kids, not to be deterred, entered her name and information on a matchmaking site. When a gentleman would call, she'd make a startling statement. "Sir, I need to tell you, I have aids!"

The Enemy Wants to Steal Our Joy

The Scripture that speaks of songs growing faint could also refer to the loss of joyful melodies as one begins to experience the challenges of aging. I'm confident God didn't intend for us to grow sad when the later years come creeping in the back door. If we determine to meditate on the Lord's blessings and provisions, the joy in our hearts can continue to swell.

Determine to Keep the Right Attitude

Sammie came to our prayer group after just going through a divorce. She'd declared bankruptcy and moved from a $600,000 home to a shed in her brother's backyard with no bathroom, running water, or even a kitchenette. A few months after she moved there, she was diagnosed with breast cancer and scheduled for a double mastectomy. Sammie calmly told our group, "God has given me great peace. I've always wanted a breast reduction, but hadn't thought of getting this drastic! But, guess what? I get to choose the size I want to be." Our eyes widened and our mouths dropped open as we were amazed at how completely she'd put her life, her faith, and her trust in God. She's a living example of how a person can adapt to life-threatening and devastating situations. She held on to the song in her heart.

Sammie put some of her things in a storage unit including a locked box filled with heirloom jewelry worth over twenty thousand dollars. A few weeks after she stored her things, she discovered the unit had been broken into and her jewelry was gone. She was upset, but sighed, "I didn't wear it much, and when I did, I was always afraid someone was going to knock me in the head and steal it. I don't have to worry about *that* anymore." I marveled. She sincerely believes *jewels* are not as important as her spiritual treasures that no one can steal.

This amazing woman now ministers full-time to the homeless, depending on the support of others who believe in what she's been called to do. She sometimes buys only a gallon of gas at a time because that's all the money she has. Once when she was driving cross-country, the gas gauge registered empty, but she drove for over sixty miles—on fumes.

She is a prime example of one who refuses to let the song in her heart fade away. She found joy by setting up a nonprofit organization, 52/52 Ministries. Sammie is content to live on a pittance, while constantly on the lookout for ways to provide for others who have nothing. She teaches the Bible to the homeless and finds great pleasure in leading them to the rich life Jesus promised. She is poor in the world's eyes, but rich in God's kingdom.

Look to God, Not Circumstances

Another friend went through a devastating trauma when her husband of eighteen years announced he'd filed for divorce. He'd found a *sweet young thing* at the office. Unfortunately, Judy had never worked outside the home because she and her husband decided she should be a stay-at-home mom. At the time, their two children were teenagers. "Not to worry," her husband assured her. "You can keep the house (with a large mortgage payment), and I'll send you $500 a month to live on."

Judy was devastated as she watched her husband drive away in a new BMW convertible. She panicked. *There's no way I'll have enough money for mortgage payments or to take care of the children on the pittance he offered to send.* Immobilized, she fell into deep depression. She sold the house for just enough equity to buy a small mobile home.

One morning, while reading the Bible, she came across the following Scripture: "A cheerful heart is good medicine, but a crushed spirit dries up the bones" (Prov. 17:22). She gasped, "I don't want dry bones!" She laid her Bible aside and slinked into her bedroom, closed the door, put on praise and worship music, and stood reaching toward the ceiling. In spite of her devastation, she mumbled, "Praise...You...Jesus... hallelujah. Thank...You...Lord." She repeated this over and over, until after a time, her shoulders began to lift and she spoke louder and with more enthusiasm. Within an hour, she was almost shouting, "Praise You, Jesus. Thank You, Lord. Hallelujah. I know You will get me through this!"

A friend called her on the phone. "You sound so upbeat; did your husband come back?"

"No, he didn't come back, but I've been talking to my Heavenly Father and He promised *He* will never leave me!" She went on to explain the miracle happened when she praised God and began to trust in His grace to stand with her through these trying times. Slowly, her prayers became a powerful force that lifted her above her circumstances. She found a job and was promoted until she could make it and take care of herself and her teenagers.

Her children are grown now, but you can always spot her glowing countenance and smile as she enters a room. She has remarried and her new husband loves her dearly and provides well for her. She still listens to praise and worship songs and hopeful chords continue to be revived in her heart.

Keep Looking up

We all have trying events that pop up, and at the time, they appear to be too hard to solve. They may come as a health problem, a financial crisis, or a bad relationship that broadsides us. In order to keep from slinking away dejected, we must learn to hold steady and look up to God. He is capable of helping us climb to spiritual heights in the most difficult of seasons.

"I look up to the mountains; does my strength come from the mountains? No, my strength comes from GOD, who made heaven, and earth, and mountains" (Ps. 121:1–2 MSG).

Years back, I prayed for joy and a sense of humor, and it was as if the Holy Spirit anointed me with the oil of joy. Laughter burst forth as a natural response.

There have been numerous times when the devil has tried to steal the joy or song in my heart, but the Lord held me steady. I refused to throw up my hands in defeat. I find bits of joy in the midst of the most difficult trials. This doesn't mean I'm never sad, but when bad things happen, I can be the first to laugh at some of my idiotic reactions. Humor is a shield I hold up against a grumpy attitude. I try to respond in the same way as the Proverb's woman: "She looks forward to the future with joy" (Prov. 31:25(Zech. 9:16–17 TLB).

I'm convinced God showed His sense of humor when He put my DNA together. For years, every time we moved to a new city, I'd determine to appear as if I had it all together—sophisticated and poised. This typically lasted about five minutes, before I'd do or say something weird, dumb, or even stupid. If I laughed first, however, others often ended up laughing and usually liked me anyway.

I prayed, "God, what is my purpose in life—why did you create me?" I felt He looked down in love and said, "Bring joy to my heart." I hope I do that on a regular basis. He has certainly brought joy to my heart.

Don't Let Other's Problems Destroy Your Joy

A few years ago, I found myself fretting over one of my sons' relationships. I had difficulty sleeping because stress bombarded me as I tried to figure out a way for the two of them to resolve their problem.

Then, I had a dream. I saw myself in the kitchen stepping in something sticky though I couldn't see anything on the floor. After the third time I stepped in it, my son came to the kitchen door and pointed to a wad of chewing gum on the floor and apologized. "I'm sorry, Mom. That's my gum, I'll clean it up."

The impact of this dream brought me to a stark realization of something I needed to confess. I'd continued to step in a sticky situation that was neither my problem nor my responsibility. A prompting from the Lord encouraged me to step back and spend quality time in prayer—to say less and pray more. The Lord always does a better job scrubbing the glue off sticky situations, so there's no need for me to get stuck in other people's business. Getting involved in their problems can destroy the songs in our heart.

Look for the Good

A young mother was having a miserable day. She hadn't dressed or combed her hair. Her two children were fighting and scattering their toys across the living room. The dog had thrown up in the middle of the floor and she hadn't had the "oomph" to clean it up. Clothes lay unfolded, piled high on the couch.

The doorbell rang. She went to the door and gasped when she saw her old boyfriend and his new bride standing there—dressed to a ten with every hair in place.

She hesitantly invited them in as she ran her fingers through her uncombed hair. The flap of her worn-out house slipper caught the edge of the carpet and caused her to stumble. The couple visited for a few minutes and left. She was mortified down to the chipped paint on her toenails and trembled as she dialed her husband at work. After she explained her horrible experience, her husband paused and then said, "Honey, that's wonderful."

She screamed into the phone. "What in the world are you talking about? I can't think of much of anything more humiliating!"

"Wait baby, listen to me. That old boyfriend will never be sorry about choosing his present wife. She will never be jealous of you, and best of all—I love you just the way you are. I'll be home early, honey, and we'll go out to eat."

110

She cradled the phone and stood there sobbing with gratitude. After cleaning up the dog vomit and picking up a few toys, she went to the kitchen, poured a cup of coffee, and sat on the couch to fold clothes and count her blessings. Her thoughtful husband made her grateful. Her heart would sing again.

Joy Deep Inside

All the staff at the retreat center had gone to town. It was late in the afternoon when I noticed an orange glow through the window shade. I opened the door and was startled to see flames of fire leaping from the barn, licking the branches of the tall pine trees behind it. I called 911 immediately and grabbed a small fire extinguisher and ran toward the flames. At that point, I imagined God smiling and whispering, "That's like trying to kill an elephant with a fly swatter!" I threw the extinguisher down and ran toward the barn to try to get the tractors, riding lawn mowers, and golf carts out of the fiery trap.

As I neared the entry, cans of gasoline began to explode. I stopped short. It was too late to risk going inside. *Thank You, Lord. You stopped me from rushing into the roaring flames. Surely You must have saved my life.*

By the time the fire department arrived, there was nothing left to salvage. The firefighters stayed for hours, continuing to put out fires that kept popping up from the bales of hay stacked in the back of the barn. Dark skeletons of tractors and equipment mocked me as a voice within whispered, "It's gone, *all* gone."

When the staff returned home, we hugged each other and cried. Paul, our director, suggested we gather in the living room of the main house. He explained, "Fire is often used as a sign of purification. Let's pray that if there's anything unclean in our lives, God will show us so we can confess and repent." He paused. "And remember, our purpose in being here is not dependent on how nice the place looks. If we have to mow a path to the front door with a push mower, we'll do that. Let's pledge to keep our focus on God and what He commissioned us to do—to reach out to hurting people with Jesus' healing touch."

The five little boys who were children of the staff had been in an adjoining bedroom praying. Adam, who was ten, was the oldest. He came in with a picture with an embroidered Scripture in his hand. "I think we need to hang this where we can see and remember what it says." The Scripture read, "And we know that God causes everything to work together for the good of those who love God and are called according to his purpose for them" (Rom. 8:28 NLT). We thanked him with hugs and tears.

When I called the insurance company, the agent told me he didn't think any part of our loss was covered, but he would send an insurance adjuster to look at the damage. A staff member questioned, "Louise, how does all this make you feel?"

It only took a moment for me to reply. "I'm sad on the outside, but deep within, I still have joy."

We turned the problem over to God and determined to move forward with our ministry. Remarkably, God showed up. The insurance adjuster came and assured us, "Of course the damage is covered. In fact, Paul paid extra premiums that included replacement value."

A few months later, we sponsored a barbeque for the purpose of an old fashioned "barn raising." Men brought their families and tools. My son, Chip, and his friends furnished live music which brought joy to our hearts. By the end of the day, great strides had been made in rebuilding the barn. Our spirits soared. We called it our "barn again" experience.

We Make Choices

Years ago, we moved into an unfinished house in Valparaiso, Indiana. We hired an older gentleman to complete the job. He constantly sang and whistled as he sawed, hammered, and painted. One day, I felt it would be good to let him know I'd noticed. "Joe, you're a joy to be around. Your singing and whistling are so upbeat."

He laid his hammer down and turned to me with a sad look in his eyes. "It hasn't always been this way. Twenty years ago, my wife and three children were coming into town. When they crossed a railroad track, they were hit by a train. All four of them were killed."

Joe wiped his forehead. "I fell into the depths of depression. I couldn't eat or sleep and couldn't talk about anything else. After six months, a friend put his arm around my shoulder and said, 'Joe, you have been through an incredible tragedy. I don't know what I'd do if I were in your shoes. You may well be depressed for the rest of your life.' He paused and then added, 'I'm sorry, my friend, but I don't think you have the right to make everyone around you miserable.' I was shocked, but his challenge cut to the bone."

Joe paused to take a sip of water. "I began to force myself to talk of other things." He sighed and continued. "I learned to whistle and began to sing. An ugly scar will always remain in my heart, but I began to live again."

"The LORD is my strength and my song; He has given me victory" (Ps. 118:14 NLT).

People Respond in Different Ways

Shortly after hearing this carpenter's story, we moved to a small West Texas town. A couple who were in their seventies attended the church where we worshipped. They always looked dejected. One day I asked another church member, "What is their problem? They look so miserable—I'll bet when they drink water, it runs out of the down-turned corners of their mouths."

My friend pressed her lips together and sighed. "Long ago, their two children were walking home from school after a flash flood. When they started across a bridge, it washed out and both of them were drowned. This couple stayed stuck in their grief. It has been the focus point of their lives." Some allow the song in their hearts to flicker and go out after tragedies or calamities.

The difference in the way people handle grief is profound. These examples made a lasting impression on me. It made me aware that I also have a choice as to how I can react to calamities. And my reaction affects every aspect of my life. If I continue to dwell on bad things, it will muffle the song in my heart. "By day the LORD directs his love, at night his song is with me" (Ps. 42:8).

Praise Brings Victory

God often sent singers and instruments ahead of the children of Israel when they went into battle. Musicians led the way as they were convicted that the battle was the Lords.

When Paul and Silas sang and prayed in prison, God responded in a beautiful way when He unlocked the prison doors as well as their chains. (See Acts 16:24-27 TLB). If there's any situation that keeps us locked behind doors of defeat or sadness, perhaps praise will cause God to set us free.

It's disheartening to see people growing older and losing their joy and optimism. I believe in the adage of "what goes around comes around." If we take time to send out showers of joy now, no doubt happiness will come back to reign on our lives.

God has the power to help us win every battle against the devil. We *can* make a choice to keep the songs of triumph from growing faint in our hearts.

> "The LORD your God is with you; he is mighty to save.
> He will take great delight in you, he will quite you with
> his love, he will rejoice over you with singing" (Zeph.
> 3:17).

We become more like Jesus when we keep listening for a song in our hearts.

LIFE APPLICATION

1. Does a hearing loss limit your ability to communicate with others?
2. If you have difficulty hearing, have you considered investing in hearing aids?
3. What can you do to lift your spirits when you're feeling discouraged?
4. Do we have the choice of being pleasant and cheerful?
5. Is it hypocritical to force yourself to act happy when you don't feel like it?
6. Can you stay optimistic in spite of tragedies in your life?
7. Think of someone who chose to be cheerful even after they'd gone through horrific trauma.
8. Do you use praise and worship music to lift your spirits?
9. Do you know someone who let a tragedy ruin their life?
10. How does faith in God give us the ability to accept the things that happen in life?

14

AVOID SOME HEIGHTS, CLIMB OTHERS

... when men are afraid of heights ...
Ecclesiastes 12:5

Unless your name is George H. W. Bush, I doubt you'll be parachuting from an airplane at age ninety. Heights are threatening to older citizens because of their lack of stability, balance, and slower reflexes. Bones, which are our support system, are also brittle and easily broken. A fall could mark the end of mobility. "When my skin sags and my bones get brittle, GOD is rock-firm and faithful" (Ps. 73:25 MSG).

An eighty-four-year-old man at church fell and broke his hip. The doctor told his wife, "It's quite possible he won't live another year." Since the man worked hard in raising a prize-winning garden and had a well-kept yard, he had firm muscles. As a result, a year later, he was fit and strong, back to his old routine of digging, weeding, and tending his large garden. The doctors pronounced him one hundred percent healed. This serves as a reminder for me to keep physically active to strengthen my bones.

Most Youth Have No Fear of Heights

I heard the young people in the backyard yelling, "Come on, Chip!" I opened the door just in time to see my son dive from the peak of our garage into the swimming pool, ten feet away. It was too late to stop him, but enough time for my heart to skip a beat. Though his friends were cheering him on, my fear went ballistic as I pictured him falling and lying lifeless beside the pool.

He assured me later, "Don't worry, Mom. I've been to Possum Kingdom where I dove into the lake from seventy-foot cliffs." Gasp! I'm thankful that now, years later, his common sense has kicked in and he is no longer so adventuresome.

Chip's uncle Don set a fearless example. He served as the ship's commander in a war zone during World War II. He dove off the mast of a ship into the ocean to prove to the ship's crew how a person could escape if they were trapped on a burning ship. Now that he's old, however, he's cautious about climbing up on a chair to change a light bulb.

Some Have Always Feared Heights

I was fearful of heights when I was young. I climbed a windmill when I was ten years old. When I was approximately two-thirds of the way to the top, I looked at the ground far below and was terrified at the thought of falling. When I looked up, clouds were blowing overhead and the windmill appeared to be falling on top of me. I white-knuckled my grip and froze as I screamed for my brother to help me. He yelled back, "Just look straight ahead and climb down, one step at a time."

That's still good advice. In life, it's wise to keep looking straight ahead and move in the right direction—one step at a time—until we come to a safe place.

Have You Fallen Lately?

A questionnaire at the doctor's office asked if I'd fallen more than once during the past year. *Nosey,* I'd fallen twice! One time I stumbled over a small rock in my son's yard; the other, I missed a six-inch step down from a curb. Six inches shouldn't strike me as a fearful height. But regardless, when I stumble, I don't want to tumble. When this old body falls, it makes one big splat.

My brother-in-law, Jim, jumped from one of the lower rungs of a ladder and crushed his heel. The doctor told him, "Anyone over seventy has no business on a ladder." As we grow older, it's wise to be more cautious, knowing a fall could easily break a bone.

Spiritually, however, God doesn't intend for us to stay on the bottom rung of the ladder. "I'm not afraid when you walk at my side" (Ps. 23:4 MSG). God expects us to continue to climb to a higher plane. "And when you draw close to God, God will draw close to you" (James 4:8 TLB). Though we're earth*born*, He doesn't intend for us to remain earth*bound*.

I went to visit my sister-in-law, Nan. When I arrived, I knocked on the door and heard a muffled plea, "Come help me!" I opened the door and found her lying on the floor. She'd fallen and couldn't get up. With a few prayers and her cooperation, we got her into a chair. Though there was no height involved, her age and weakness caused her to lose her balance while simply walking across the room. She thanked me several times, "I don't know what I'd done if you hadn't come." Thankfully, the Lord arranged for me to arrive at the right time.

Sometimes, we trip on the stairway to heaven, but God only counts our mistakes as failure if we refuse to get up. We're to keep climbing. Our journey is not an escalator. We can't stand in one place and think we'll be automatically lifted to the top.

Pride

One thing that is more dangerous than physical height is thinking more highly of ourselves than we ought to think. The Lord has no tolerance for pride because pride relies on self rather than God. "Don't be so naive and self-confident. You're not exempt. You could fall flat on your face as easily as anyone else" (1 Cor. 10:12 MSG).

In the background we may hear the devil mock and harasses us about our weakened condition as age tromps across our bodies. But God would have us use aging as a time to deal with pride. During this season, Satan counts on us becoming discouraged and losing hope because we can't function as well as we once did. Every speck of pride may be blasted because "this old gray mare ain't what she used to be." But the things Satan plans for evil, God can use for good. There are times when we may have to ask for help, which is humbling, though essential. We may need assistance—time and again. God invites us to depend more on Him and those who are stronger than we are.

Even through we're not as capable as we once were, the Father can still use us to accomplish great things.

> "God chose things the world considers foolish in order to shame those who think they are wise. And he chose things that are powerless to shame those who are powerful" (1 Cor. 1:27 NLT).

Hey! Those of us who feel powerless may be chosen by God.

Consider King David, the youngest and smallest of his family. He depended on God. He set an incredible example of faith when he faced that huge giant with only a small slingshot as a weapon. He trusted God to win this battle even though most in the Israelite army were older and more experienced.

God also chose Gideon, who felt inadequate and argued with God about picking him to lead a small group of soldiers to win a major battle.

When God uses unlikely people, they know it has to be God who accomplishes the work. Since God chooses weak people, why wouldn't He choose older people?

Run the Race

Our lack of confidence may keep us from accomplishing what we're capable of doing. Many years ago, the athletic world concluded no man would ever run the mile in less than four minutes. A mental block made it appear impossible. But there were those who made this the height of their ambition. An Englishman, Roger Bannister, burst the imaginary bubble in 1954. After Roger's breakthrough, an American, Steve Scott, ran the sub-four-minute-mile 186 times. Not only that, but an Irishman, Eanonn Goglin, was the first man over forty to shatter the four-minute-mile myth. (Perhaps he could do that because he was over the hill, age-wise, and on a downhill slope!)

God's Purpose Shows Up in Many Ways

A neighbor became incapacitated with a number of strains of arthritis. Ultimately, she was confined to her bed, scarcely able to move any part of her body.

Her husband rigged up a phone with a headset so she could continue her ministry of counseling and mentoring people all over the world. Even with the inability to walk or get out of bed, she continued to climb higher in serving God and others. She explained, "I can endure the pain as long as God can use me in some way."

When she believed the end was near, she urged her family to build a simple pine box to bury her in. She asked to be carried by pallbearers she had carried spiritually. She was unable to climb here, but in death, I'm sure she ascended to the heights.

God Searches for the Obedient

God is watching and waiting to help those who walk in obedience. The Lord searches throughout the earth to find those who have fallen—to those who admit they can't make it alone. He reaches down and lifts them so they can stand strong. *Pick us up and dust us off, Lord. We dare not fear the heights because You're willing to help us keep moving toward heaven.*

It is incredible to think of being seated in heaven with Christ Jesus. "Since you have been raised to new life with Christ, set your sights on the realities of heaven, where Christ sits in the place of honor at God's right hand" (Col. 3:1 NLT).

If we are seated with Christ, we ought to be able to look down and see things from His perspective. Every trial offers us an opportunity for our love and confidence to grow deeper. This is the height I'd like to be lifted to!

Those Who Follow

There are younger and stronger pilgrims following us. I have grandchildren who are spiritually light-years ahead of where I was at their age. I'm excited about passing the baton to this next generation. Though I may not be able to go where they go, I can help support them. "Lord, let my money, prayers and encouragement be like water and sunlight, empowering them to go and grow." We cheer them on, praying they'll climb higher and possibly bring about the worldwide revival we long for. "Don't let anyone think less of you because you are young. Be an example to all believers in what you say, in the way you live, in your love, your faith, and your purity" (1 Tim. 4:12 NLT).

A Little Child Shall Lead Them

My granddaughter, Belle, was only five when she taught us a lesson on prayer. Since her folks live in the Gulf Coast area of Texas, they seldom see even tiny flecks of snow. At Thanksgiving, when they went to their cabin in Colorado, Belle prayed for snow. That year they only had a light sprinkling, so when they went back in the spring, Belle prayed, "Lord, send a lot of snow." As they neared the cabin, they were met with near blizzard conditions. The snow drifts became so high their van got stuck, and they had to hike a half mile through deep snow to get to the cabin." Belle was riding on her dad's shoulders and kept apologizing over and over. "Daddy, I'm so sorry I prayed for too much snow."

On their next trip, she prayed for *some* snow. After a couple of days of clear weather, her father consoled her, "Belle, I'm sorry, but it looks as if your prayer won't get answered this time."

"Don't worry, Daddy, God is probably answering someone else's prayer." Is it a wonder we're to become like little children? Belle looked beyond her own desires for snow to others that might be praying for it not to snow.

Interestingly, that afternoon and evening, they were blessed with a beautiful blanket of snow. How delightful that the Lord of heaven and earth sometimes chooses a child, rather than a rocket scientist, to teach us. *Reach to God, little one. Seek His higher plane.*

Belle is now fourteen and has been supporting an orphan in a third world country for a year. She works at small jobs to raise the money needed to feed a starving child. She has expressed her desire to someday go to Africa to work in an orphanage. For her fourteenth birthday, she had a party and asked guests to bring money, rather than gifts, to help those in desperate situations. In all, she was able to raise $1,250 to send to Compassion International to feed starving children.

Do You Look Like Jesus?

One year, before seatbelts were required, we were traveling and three-year-old Kathy sat in my lap. She looked out the window toward the sky and said, "I think I see Jesus."

Curious, I asked, "What does He look like?"

She paused a moment before she answered. "I think He looks like my daddy."

Wouldn't it be wonderful if people were reminded of Jesus when they looked at us? Let your imaginations run wild—like that of a child. Look to the heavens in anticipation of the soon-coming Lord to take us home to live with Him forever

Think of a small child reaching up and saying, "Hold me." Only a hard heart could resist that tender request. In the same way, I believe we can also reach up to our Heavenly Father with the humble request, "Hold me." We're assured—as we draw near to our Father, He will draw near to us. "Defend your people, Lord; defend and bless your chosen ones. Lead them like a shepherd and carry them forever in your arms" (Ps. 28:9 TLB).

How exciting to think of our Majestic God riding through the heavens on the clouds and watching to see who will reach out to Him. "He rides across the heavens to help you, across the skies in majestic splendor. The eternal God is your refuge, and his everlasting arms are under you" (Deut. 33:26–27 NLT). It's time for us to lose our fear of heights and fly high with Him.

Jesus draws us to Himself. Our attitudes and demeanor will likely cause others to want to draw near the God we serve.

We Need to Aspire to Some Higher Places

Jesus led His chosen three to the Mount of Transfiguration and gave them a glimpse of the glory of God—what it will be like at the time of resurrection. Through various scriptures, we've been given a glimpse of this mountaintop experience which should sustain us during difficult days.

An old hymn by Johnson Oatman, Jr. flitters across my mind.

> *Lord, lift me up and let me stand,*
> *By faith, on Heaven's tableland.*
> *A higher plane than I have found;*
> *Lord, plant my feet on higher ground.*

I pray God will keep my feet from dragging along and bogging down in the cares of this world.

The apostle John had a vision of standing before an open door in heaven with Jesus encouraging him to come up higher so he could show him what would happen. Although we may not have any idea of what is coming in the days ahead, Scripture tells us it will be more wonderful than we can imagine.

> "I looked, and there before me was a door standing open
> in heaven. And the voice I had first heard speaking to me
> like a trumpet said, 'Come up here, and I will show you
> what must take place after this'" (Rev. 4:1–2).

Stay Prepared

The Bible tells us we don't know the day or the hour when Jesus will return. And none of us know when He will call us home. One day Jesus will shout, "Ready or not, here I come." Now is the time of preparation. The door of the elevator is opening, and, as an elevator operator used to ask, "Going up?"

LIFE APPLICATION

1. Have you fallen in recent years? If so, were you hurt?
2. Are you becoming more cautious when you are moving about?
3. Do you spend too much time thinking of the past and future while failing to pay little attention to the present?
4. Are you hesitant to do things that seem a little more difficult than usual?
5. Are you limited by what you think you can do?
6. Has age affected your confidence and pride?
7. Do you look for ways you can reach out to others?
8. Have you asked God to show you things from His perspective?
9. Do you graciously accept help when you need it?
10. Do you know of ways you can climb higher in your walk with the Lord?

15

I DON'T GET AROUND MUCH ANY MORE

... dangers in the streets ...
Ecclesiastes 12:5

As time marches on, there's a tendency for people to "roll up the sidewalks'" when it gets dark. They are afraid to venture out at night. With hearing and eyesight fading, reflexes slower, and unstable balance and weakness, they are fearful of what could happen outside in the dark.

Some people begin to withdraw socially and cut back on former activities. Those who have lost a spouse tell others they feel like a "fifth wheel" when they're with other couples, and they're not comfortable going out alone. Still others find it's too much trouble to get dressed. It takes determination to refuse to become a recluse by not going out to serve and mingle with others.

Some Shut Themselves Off from the World

A couple's daughter was killed when she and her boyfriend were involved in an accident and the car burst into flames. The boyfriend got out but didn't appear to make an attempt to rescue their daughter. The parents blamed him for their daughter's death.

In the depth of their sorrow, her parents pulled the shades in their home and isolated themselves, only going out when it was absolutely necessary. The house became like a tomb for the living dead, with little evidence of life. Tragically, the giant spider of agoraphobia trapped this couple inside its sticky web.

If you find yourself pulling away, you may have to get behind yourself and push to get away from the confines of your home. "We throw open our doors to God and discover at the same moment that he has already thrown open his door to us. We find ourselves standing where we always hoped we might stand—out in the wide open spaces of God's grace and glory" (Rom. 5:2 MSG). God invites us to discover life outside our constrictive environment.

When people are isolated, they tend to only be concerned with themselves and their circumstances. Their world begins to shrink. They no longer contribute to a society they were once a part of. Selfishness and self-pity may move into their spare bedroom.

Fear on the Streets

When I taught in a maximum security prison, inmates sometimes asked, "Aren't you afraid to come in here to teach?"

I smiled. "I'm probably as safe here as I would be on the streets of nearby Houston." They nodded in agreement.

I admit it was sobering when I had to sign a release: "If you are ever taken hostage, there will be no deals or ransoms." I went there day after day, refusing to be a prisoner of fear. "The fear of man brings a snare, but whoever leans on, trusts in, and puts his confidence in the Lord is safe and set on high" (Prov. 29:25 AMP).

The prison was filled with con artists, and possibly if there'd been a prison break, some inmates might have turned on me. But I sincerely believed there were those who would have died for me.

Other Dangers in the Streets

In a support group I attend, a lady who'd lived on the streets of Houston for seven years, addicted to crack cocaine, joined our group.

She slept in a tent and made her living selling drugs. Her appearance was a reflection of the hard life she lived. She had a couple of front teeth missing and a glass eye.

She'd grown weary of her lifestyle and had a burning desire to escape from this miserable existence and find a better way to live. She visited the church where we met, and they found temporary housing for her while they researched for a rehab center that would take her.

She was admitted to a Christian program that has a high rate of recovery for those with addictions. I'm confident this lady will come out of this eighteen-month program with a powerful testimony. She'll be equipped to help change the lives of others who live in danger on the streets where she was once trapped.

Most of us have never experienced life on the streets, but the nightly news keeps us abreast of evils lurking there. A police officer spoke to a group of us and warned us of predators stalking vulnerable women at night—especially those of us who are older.

Some precautions we might take:

1. Walk out of a store and stay in plain sight in the middle of parking lanes until you reach your car.
2. Don't park beside an enclosed van.
3. Be aware of schemes and scams that ask for your social security or credit card number, or the number of your bank account.
4. Report the loss of your credit card immediately.
5. If you're coming out of a store at night, find someone to walk with you or ask a security guard to watch you until you get to your car.
6. Keep the doors of your car and home locked, even during the day.
7. Wasp spray is a better deterrent than mace. (You may want to keep a can on the nightstand by your bed, by the front door, and/or in your car.)
8. Be aware of anyone that appears to be following or watching you.

9. Keep your cell phone accessible, and have at least one number you can speed-dial.
10. Never turn your back when your purse is in your shopping cart.

I was attending a seminar late one evening and had to park a distance from the auditorium. A young man on a bicycle was following me slowly. He moved from across the street and approached me from behind. He appeared to be sneaking up to snatch my purse. There were people walking a distance ahead, and I called loudly, "Wait for me." When they turned to look back, the young man sped away on his bicycle.

Times Have Changed

We don't dare leave the doors of our homes unlocked or our keys in our car. We no longer live in an era where a handshake is as binding as a legal document.

It's sad, because crime has become rampant and seniors are particularly vulnerable. We were brought up to trust people, so we've become prime targets for scams, con artists, and scheming predators with glib tongues. Identity theft has become a threat to everyone.

Dangers are not only on the streets—they now lurk inside our homes. Countless conniving and heartless people sneak into our homes via television, telephones, and the internet. Tempting offers show up in our mailboxes, appearing to be from those who are interested in our wellbeing. Their appeals tempt us, either by offering money and perks or by touching our compassionate hearts by urging us to donate to "wonderful" charities. It is sad that we need to be skeptical.

Experience has led me to make it a practice of donating only to those I *know* represent legitimate charities, as well as checking to see how much of a donation goes to administrators. I favor donating to friends and acquaintances that raise their own support and are under the umbrella of a legitimate ministry.

Don't Be Afraid to Go Alone

A few days before my husband died, a friend who leads trips to Israel called. Carey asked him to conduct his funeral and take me with his group on his next trip which was coming in a couple of months. About six weeks before our departure date, I fell and broke my ankle by tumbling down an incline in front of a grocery store. My leg was in a cast when I went back to the store a few days later and located the manager. I suggested they put a yellow stripe, a railing, or some type of warning on the edge of the ramp. He cringed. "We just talked about that in a meeting last week. We'll take care of all your expenses."

I shook my head. "That won't be necessary. I have insurance, and I have no intention of suing."

"Wait!" He said. "That's the reason we carry insurance. I'll send an adjuster to your home."

The adjuster came and filled out all the papers concerning the accident. A few weeks later, someone from the insurance company called. "Can you come to our office and pick up your check?"

"I'd be happy to," I replied. "And I can come right away." When I arrived, they handed me an envelope and I thanked them.

The agent cocked his head. "Aren't you going to open it?"

"Oh, sure," I answered as I ripped open the envelope. I gasped when I saw the amount. "This is far more than my expenses. I think you made a mistake."

He smiled. "No, but we've never had anyone try to talk us out of giving them money. You've been most gracious. Go buy yourself some new clothes for the trip." The check was enough to pay for my trip *and* buy new clothes.

I'd been out of my cast only a few days when it was time for our flight to Israel, so I moved cautiously. When we arrived, the group decided to go through Hezekiah's famous tunnel that brought water into the city of Jerusalem. It was dug seven hundred years before Christ. Water still trickles through the tunnel— over stones and uneven ground. Some questioned my decision to go through the tunnel, but one member of the tour group offered to walk beside me and hold me steady. It's always a comfort to have someone to lean on when we're going through rough places in life.

Jesus is always there for us to depend on, but it's good to have flesh and blood to support us when we could possibly stumble and fall. It removes much of the fear from the danger in the streets.

Are There Other Dangers on the Streets?

My dad was not a safe driver. He was blind in one eye and so crippled with arthritis, his reflexes were slow. Often, instead of paying attention to the road, he was looking at livestock and crops growing in the fields nearby. Sometimes he would meander into the opposite lane. It was amazing he only had a few minor accidents. Nevertheless, He was a danger on the streets.

Sadly, there are many drivers today who are filled with road rage. One night I was driving and came up too close to a pickup before I dimmed my lights. He blasted his horn and hit his brakes and I almost rear-ended him. When I passed him, he rode my bumper regardless of how fast I drove. He started to pass me and began edging over close, to force me off the road into the ditch. I was blessed when a car approached from over a hill and he had to drop back to avoid a head-on collision. Convinced he wanted to kill me, I floor-boarded the accelerator to get out of there.

Pray for God's Direction

It's time to pay close attention to God's leading. "See if there is any offensive way in me, and lead me in the way everlasting" (Ps. 139:24). On our way to walk on streets of gold, we need to ask God to remove any dangers that might block our way. And listen for God's marching orders and encourage others to join us. "Walk out of the gates. Get going! Get the road ready for the people. Build the highway. Get at it! Clear the debris, hoist high a flag, a signal to all peoples!" (Isa. 62:10 MSG). This will take care of any fear in the streets.

LIFE APPLICATION

1. Are you staying closer to home than you did in times past? If so, what are your reasons?
2. Do you invite other seniors to come along when you go out?
3. Are you so independent you won't allow others to help when you need them?
4. Do you think others should take care of you now?
5. What precautions do you take when you're out in public?
6. How do you protect your identity, such as your social security number, driver's license, and credit cards?
7. Are you willing to help others who are physically weaker?
8. Do you spend too much time thinking only of yourself and your own circumstances?
9. Do you listen when others suggest you curtail some of your activities?
10. Do your limitations frustrate you?

16

IF I'M LIKE A TREE, LET ME BEAR FRUIT

... when the almond tree blossoms ...
Ecclesiastes 12:5

An almond tree with white blossoms is likely Solomon's description of someone with white hair. Pink blossoms on an almond tree indicate its almonds will be bitter. Almond trees with white blossoms have sweet almonds. I'm hoping that our white hair indicates we'll be sweet *nuts*.

Some find a few gray hairs sprouting in their early forties and may be reminded of the words of an old song by Eben E. Rexford, "Darling, we are growing old—silver threads among the gold." Some pluck the offending hairs for a time before deciding they'd rather have gray hair than no hair at all.

Some dye their hair to keep the gray from showing. Not many agree with Solomon when he wrote that the gray hair of wisdom was more beautiful than the strength of young people.

Although I'm white-headed, I hope it's not a sign that all the color has drained from my life.

Hair Problems

At God's appointed time, an almond tree loses its blossoms. Some people lose their hair because of genetics. Other losses come as the result of medication. When my husband, Carey, had cancer and took chemo, his hair came out by the handfuls. As he stood in front of the mirror one morning, he grinned, "Since God knows the number of hairs on our head, it must take an angel full time to keep up with mine. He probably just now had to subtract at least another hundred." Carey stared at his brush and shook his head. "I used to have a crew cut, but now the crew is bailing out." I couldn't resist saying, "I suppose it's just a matter of hair today, gone tomorrow."

As we accept gray hair as a telltale sign of aging, we may playfully tease our children. "I earned every one of these gray hairs, and you did your part in egging them on."

Lessons from Fruit-Bearing Trees

The almond tree's fruit has always been regarded as a valuable crop. In ancient times, almonds were symbolic of watchfulness and promise. It would be wise for us to become more watchful of our words and actions as we blossom with age.

Flowers on a fruit tree indicate fruit is on its way. The fruit ripening in this season of life may be different from fruit in earlier years, but is nonetheless important.

The Master Gardener not only intends for us to continue to bear fruit, but He also waters, prunes, and cares for us so we can be more productive. "You did not choose me, but I chose you and appointed you to go and bear fruit—fruit that will last" (John 15:16).

A Gnarled Old Pear Tree

In her early forties, my mother-in-law was left almost penniless as a widow with five children, including a baby only a few weeks old.

With the little dab of insurance money she got, she bought a small two-bedroom, cracker-box style home for her family. In the front yard, there was an ugly, old gnarled pear tree with broken limbs and a twisted shape. She wanted the eyesore cut down, but no one offered to remove it, and she didn't have the money to pay someone to do the job. The first year, it bore a few pears, so the next year she watered and fertilized it and was pleasantly surprised when the old tree yielded a bumper crop.

Each successive year, it appeared unlikely the tree would survive another season. Amazingly, it thrived. "Mom" made hundreds of jars of pear preserves and created a recipe for a pear relish people almost fought to get. These jars became standard gifts for friends and family for the remaining fifty years she lived in that home.

We May Not Look Good

Like Mom's old pear tree, we too may look like the dickens, but we can continue to bear fruit. Our skin may look like a wrinkled old prune, but I refuse to think of a prune being the fruit of the Spirit for God's older children. But like a prune, I'll just consider my wrinkles to be a sign of condensed sweetness.

Our goal should be to continue to bear the fruit of the Spirit: love, joy, peace, patience, kindness, goodness, faithfulness, gentleness, and self-control (Gal. 5:22–23). Roots of bitterness should be yanked out to keep bad fruit from thriving.

Since God grafted us into His vine, we draw strength from Him. The seeds of righteousness at the core of our being can bear good fruit for future generations.

It takes careful and severe pruning for a grapevine to bear its best fruit. As we stay connected to Jesus, who is the vine, God wants to prune off the pride, anger, and bad attitudes the enemy grafts onto the vine.

If we attempt to grow fruit on our own, we'll be like a severed limb, a dead stick on the ground—a lifeless branch which will never sprout or grow into a tree.

God Looks for Beauty on the Inside

Poochy stomachs and wrinkles don't disqualify us from becoming more beautiful inside than Miss America. We can be put on stage at all ages as the Lord's model children.

Johnny Appleseed

John Chapman, better known as Johnny Appleseed, dreamed of a country of blossoming apple trees where no one would ever go hungry. He spent the bulk of his adult life walking through New England, planting apple trees along the way. Two hundred years later, seeds from subsequent trees still bear apples.

We're commissioned to scatter seeds of the gospel, so no one ever needs to be spiritually hungry. Nothing is needed more than this good news in our troubled world. "And those who are peacemakers will plant seeds of peace and reap a harvest of righteousness" (James 3:18 NLT).

As seed-planters, we're to be on the lookout for fertile soil everywhere we go. We have the responsibility to teach others about the saving grace of Jesus.

Plow Hard Ground

Soil is tilled to keep it from becoming hardened and packed. Plowed ground holds the moisture and allows the sun and air to get to the seeds so they will sprout and grow.

> "Sow for yourselves righteousness reap the fruit of unfailing love, and break up your unplowed ground; for it is time to seek the LORD, until he comes and showers righteousness on you" (Hos. 10:12).

Eating the Wrong Fruit

In the Garden of Eden, Eve was attracted to the forbidden fruit growing on the tree of good and evil. It was beautiful and looked delicious. Satan encouraged her to eat it and lied by telling her she wouldn't die if she ate it. He deceived her by saying the fruit would make her like God and she would know good and evil. Before Adam and Eve ate the fruit, they only knew *good* as God walked and talked with them in the cool of the evening.

When this first couple ate the poisonous fruit, it opened a doorway to death as God had forewarned. Any time one does what he wants rather than obeying God, he chooses a pathway that can lead to the death of his soul.

The curse of doing our own thing passed from one generation to the next. It was expressed in the song Frank Sinatra sang, "I Did It My Way." This arrogant attitude destroys our relationship with the Lord.

We Can Be Wise

True wisdom doesn't come from impressive academic degrees or books, but rather as a godly gift. James, the brother of Jesus, gave us the good news that God gives wisdom to those who ask. And our Father never considers an honest question to be dumb or stupid.

God doesn't compromise truth. He's not interested in being politically correct. When we waffle back and forth trying to decide who we'll listen to, we're compared to a wave of the sea tossed about and awash with confusion.

Hopefully, we've gained some wisdom over the years. It would be pathetic if we've failed to gain some insight along the way. "Is not wisdom found among the aged? Does not long life bring understanding?" (Job 12:12).

Wonderful Trees

The Word speaks of the Tree of Life in Revelation. It is pictured as growing on each side of the River of Life, bearing new crops every month of the year. Its green leaves are His prescription to heal the nations. It's free, cures every disease, and has no small print that lists bad side effects.

Near the gate of our retreat center stood a huge oak tree that opened its arms to welcome every guest. I prayed for this old tree when hurricanes headed in from the Gulf. *Hang in there, old fellow. Dig in your roots. Don't let winds or storms topple you.*

We, too, can lift our arms and offer comfort to those who are going through emotional storms, praying the assaults won't cause them to fall on their face. We are to be oaks of righteousness, planted beside streams of water, whose roots grow deep into Jesus' love. "They will be called oaks of righteousness, a planting of the LORD for the display of his splendor" (Isa. 61:3). The winds of adversity will not uproot us, and long periods of drought will not cause us to wilt. We'll continue to bear fruit as long as we're tapped into the Water of Life.

What a beautiful plan God has for us. "Even to your old age and gray hairs I am he, I am he who will sustain you. I have made you and I will carry you; I will sustain you and I will rescue you" (Isa. 46:4). Mom kept her old pear tree because it continued to produce good fruit. Won't God sustain us as we continue to bear good fruit?

I'd love for the leaves growing on the branches of my life to offer healing to the emotional hurts and pain of those who battle discouragement.

LIFE APPLICATION

1. How do you feel about your body as it grows older?
2. How might you continue to grow and bear good fruit?
3. Do you have roots of anger or bitterness that need to be pulled out?
4. Are you sending deeper roots into the Word of God to tap into His wisdom and truth?
5. Are you scattering seed in the lives of younger people so they can continue to bear fruit long after you're gone?
6. Do you offer your arms of comfort and encouragement to those who are hurting?
7. Are you more interested in looking good or being good?
8. In what ways have you been pruned by God?
9. Do you risk spoiling a good relationship because you think you're always right?
10. How can God use you in healing the hurts of others?

17

WHO DRAINED MY ENERGY TANK?

... the grasshopper drags himself along ...
Ecclesiastes 12:5

Autumn is the time of year when it appears nature is slowing down to take a long, deep breath. The trees relax and drop leaves like giant brown snowflakes, floating down to snuggle close to the warm earth. Ah! Breathe deeply and allow the cares of the world to slide from your shoulders.

However, the fall season of life does have a way of siphoning strength and energy from our bodies. In spite of all our efforts to keep this physical body strong, inevitably, it grows weary. We experience our own energy crisis. I find myself huffing and puffing after going up one flight of stairs. As I grow older and move slower, I thank God He doesn't run off and leave me behind.

We Can Become Stronger

We can regain, or at least stall, some waning physical energy by exercising. It's encouraging to know many muscles can be rebuilt or strengthened at any age. Jack LaLane, an exercise guru, continued his exercise routine well into his nineties. Scripture agrees that physical exercise is good for the body. However, it also tells us that spiritual exercise is even more beneficial for the soul.

There are YMCA's and senior exercise programs in many communities. In our subdivision, we have an eighty-three-year-old woman who leads water aerobics. I enjoy her classes so much, I make it a priority to attend regularly. Psychologists suggest that exercise not only improves zapped energy, it can also strengthen us emotionally by lifting our spirits.

Joy Can Be Energizing

Over the years, I've kept the welcome mat out as an invitation for those who were stressed out, worn out, or just want to come for a visit. I have to admit, there are times when I do get tired.

One day I breathed a sigh of relief as I waved good-bye to a group. Suddenly, I remembered more guests were on their way and I'd told them I'd have supper ready for them. I had nothing to prepare.

I grumbled as I drove to the store to buy groceries. Weariness nipped at my heels as I got out of the car and grabbed a cart to lean on for support. When I realized where my thoughts were taking me, I threw back my shoulders and began to repeat, "The joy of the Lord is my strength." I deliberately quickened my step and spoke cheerfully to a woman heading to her car with a stash of groceries. Before I finished shopping, I felt much better because the Lord rewarded me with a portion of His joyous strength. I even became excited about seeing the friends who were coming for dinner.

Tiredness Versus Weariness

Tiredness and weariness are different. Hard work may wear us down physically, but we usually feel revitalized after a good night's sleep. I call that a *good tired*. Weariness affects us emotionally and seeps deep in our bones, settling in through the long hours of the night. We're still not rested or energized the following morning.

When we're weary, our faces usually reflect telltale signs of despondency. Discouragement is sculpted on our faces. Our shoulders droop, and the sparkle in our eyes fades, announcing to the world, "We're frazzled."

Moods are often detected by our tone of voice. Weariness is evident in the first word my friend speaks when she answers the phone. You know her emotions have bottomed out when she responds with a slow and mournful, "Hel—lo."

I'm confident we can reverse the curse of looking and sounding weary. A good place to start is with a cheerful voice. When we sound upbeat, our bodies are apt to follow suit and our shoulders begin to lift.

Don't Drag Around!

The word "drag" could form a negative acronym to remind us to not be like an old grasshopper dragging itself around.

D – droopy
R – resigned
A – apathetic
G – grumpy

Our bodies may be weary and weak, but our spirits can keep on hopping. Who knows? Some of that inner energy is likely to spill over into the physical realm. By God's grace, we will be revitalized and upbeat.

A smile reflects a cheerful heart and is contagious. When we smile, people of all ages perk up and often smile in response. Smiles can be a trigger releasing a bullet of joy that happily explodes on those surrounding us. Then, we not only cheer others—joy drips off our chins and waters our own souls.

The Recipe for Happiness

Father God, help us mature to the point that we can join the apostle Paul in his declaration:

"I've learned by now to be quite content whatever my

circumstances. I'm just as happy with little as with much.... I've found the recipe for being happy whether full or hungry, hands full or hands empty. Whatever I have, wherever I am, I can make it through anything in the One who makes me who I am" (Phil. 4:11–13 MSG).

The apostle reminds us we can choose to be content in every situation.

God's Word Is Strengthening

Heavy loads become lighter when we rely on the truths of God's promises. I find it helpful to tape uplifting scriptures on my bathroom mirror and read them regularly. Better still, we can memorize meaningful Bible verses. However, they can be written on notecards to carry in our pocket to read aloud when we have bits of time.

The most difficult trials usually reveal either our greatest strengths or our greatest weaknesses. Take note of emotions that float to the surface when a situation turns sour.

I have to admit it's hard to stay patient when the road is longer and harder than I anticipated. I've found it to be helpful to do things for others. Some days I start off tired and not in the mood to do much of anything. I have to get behind myself and push to get jump-started. But if I do something for someone else, I find it uncovers a fresh battery of strength to get recharged.

When our children were small, we knew a family that was struggling financially. One night, we bought bags of groceries to leave on their front porch. Our little ones rang the doorbell and scurried into the bushes to hide. We watched from a distance as the family opened the door and looked around to try to find who'd blessed them. That outreach was like a shot of adrenalin for us. We chuckled and were energized every time we thought about what we'd done.

The Lord Never Gets Tired

If anyone ever had a reason to be weary, God does. Can you imagine

His looking down on the dismal way His children have blown it through lack of respect, sin, and selfishness? It's difficult to understand how, after centuries of dealing with unfaithful children, He doesn't hurl us into outer darkness.

> "Don't you know? Haven't you heard? The LORD is the eternal God, Creator of the earth. He never gets weary or tired his wisdom cannot be measured. The LORD gives strength to those who are weary" (Isa. 40:28–29 CEV).

The Lord infuses His strength into our worn-out knees and sagging spirits. It's time to tell our bodies to get up and get on with life. I don't understand why God is so patient with us, but I'm forever grateful.

> "I've been carrying you on my back from the day you were born, and I'll keep on carrying you when you're old. I'll be there, bearing you when you're old and gray" (Isa. 46:3–4 MSG).

God blesses us by refreshing us, energizing every cell in our bodies. We dare not wander far from God because He is our ultimate strength.

> "Are you tired? Worn out? Burned out on religion? Come to me. Get away with me and you'll recover your life. I'll show you how to take a real rest. Walk with me and work with me—watch how I do it. Learn the unforced rhythms of grace. I won't lay anything heavy or ill-fitting on you. Keep company with me and you'll learn to live freely and lightly" (Matt. 11:28–30 MSG).

As we grow older and move more slowly, we can be thankful our Lord adjusts His pace to stay close to us. He orchestrates simple rhythms of grace and invites us to dance. Like an old tree in the wind, I creak a bit when I sway, but I'm pleased to see Him smiling His approval as He stands nearby and watches me.

LIFE APPLICATION

1. Do you get discouraged because you have less energy than you once did?
2. Do you have an exercise program to help you stay energized?
3. If you are depressed or weary, can you think of things you might do to recover?
4. Does your tone of voice sound upbeat?
5. What are the things you talk about most?
6. What can you do to help change negative conversations?
7. Do you consciously try to be cheerful and kind?
8. Have you learned to be content in every situation you find yourself in?
9. Would it help if you knew others were cheering you on your journey?
10. Have you reached out to help someone recently?

18

HAVE YOUR DESIRES FADED?

... desire no longer is stirred ...
Ecclesiastes 12:5

Some consider this *desire* Solomon speaks of as applying to sexuality. Though this is possibly what he alluded to, there are other desires related to age that fade, such as our hopes and dreams.

As we grow older, we tend to burn out, rust out, or wear out. Those burned out may say, "I'm sick and tired of it all." Those who rust out may sit down to rest and, like the Tin Man in the Wizard of Oz, stay stuck so long they squeak when forced to move. *Thank You, Lord, that Your Holy Spirit is like anointing oil we need to loosen us up.* (It beats WD-40 any time.) "How wonderful, how beautiful, when brothers and sisters get along! It's like costly anointing oil flowing down head and beard" (Ps. 133:1−2 MSG). This isn't an appealing picture of oil dripping all over, but if it represents the flow of the oil of the Holy Spirit, I'm shouting, "Bring it on! Loosen me up and keep me moving."

Keep Hope Alive in Difficult Times

It is difficult to keep your dreams from being shattered and your hopes from evaporating when it feels like you've been punched in the pit of your stomach. At times, we need God to help us catch our breath. In one instance, I was tempted to throw up my hands and quit when I was faced with what appeared to be an intolerable situation. My dream of faithfulness in marriage was gone. I had to cling to God to keep from running, even when God whispered, "Hold steady."

Carey got involved with another woman because he allowed his desires to shift. The flattery and flirting of an older college student enticed him. When I became aware of this affair, I almost cratered. I sobbed, took a long, deep breath and remembered my marriage vows to him—"for richer or poorer, for better or worse." This surely was a part of the "worse." In a strange way, repeating my commitment somehow knocked the teeth out of the enemy's attack and sucked a portion of the poison from my wounds.

Though there were times I considered leaving and shredding my marriage license, deep within there was a burning desire to fulfill my dream of a good marriage even if Carey wasn't particularly interested. I struggled. Our children were probably the main reason I didn't bail out.

I knew unforgiveness was the number-one cause for divorce, so I decided I had to approach the problem from that angle. The enemy kept whispering, "He doesn't deserve forgiveness." That seemed true, but it didn't relieve me of my responsibility to ask God to help me forgive, knowing I continued to need God's forgiveness for the ways I'd messed up.

The hurt and pain took time to heal, but I continued to cling to my commitment. The children and I are so glad I did.

> He built a wall to shut me out,
> With bricks of rejection, pain and doubt.
> But forgiveness and love were determined to win—
> We drew a circle that brought him in.

Over twenty years later, on our thirty-fifth anniversary, Carey wrote me a letter only six months before he died. It said all I had wanted to hear him say years before. He wrote that he believed God picked me for him. He mentioned things he'd done and failed to do that could have destroyed our marriage. Included in his list of affirmations was an appreciation for my forgiving spirit. This assured me I had done the right thing when I determined to keep my marriage vows.

Some Dreams Have Faded

Some desires become unlikely or abandoned because our abilities are now limited. Hope that once rose over the horizon appears to be going down with the sunset of life. We long for the hope of tomorrow. Though everything in this life will wear out, rust out, or be thrown out, we can be restored, renewed, and rewarded when we complete the plans Almighty God has for us here, "being confident of this, that he who began a good work in you will carry it on to completion until the day of Christ Jesus" (Phil. 1:6).

Love Need Never Fade

Love can continue growing stronger and it can be expressed in different ways. My sister's mother-in-law could hardly make ends meet as an extremely poor widow. Not wanting to accept money from her children, she took in boarders and sold homemade loaves of bread. She also supplemented her income by washing and ironing businessmen's white shirts. My sister paid her to iron her husband's shirts. One day, Sis apologized. "I'm so sorry you have to do all this ironing." Her mother-in-law turned slowly and smiled. "You don't know how much love I can iron into my son's shirts." Her desire to express love to her family remained strong.

This is an ideal time of life to enlarge our tents of love. Love can be a shelter, a place of comfort from the heat and pressures of daily living. We can stretch it wide as a protection from the storms of our life and the lives of others. "Enlarge the place of your tent, stretch your tent curtains wide, do not hold back; lengthen your cords, strengthen your stakes" (Isa. 54:2 MSG).

There Are Those Who Need Someone to Care for Them

When I taught in prison, some of the inmates told me I acted as if I really cared for them. I assured them I did. I asked if they had others who loved and cared for them. Several responded, "I don't think I ever had anyone who cared whether I lived or died." My heart ached. This reminded me to make it a point to share love and encouragement with those I met—even those whose actions didn't seem to merit my love.

Those who deserve our love the least may actually need it the most. We can speak to them by phone, email, letters, or text messages. We'll never know how much small gestures may touch and change lives. Love should never fade or grow dim. I do not know of anyone who doesn't have a desire for others to love them.

Bigger Goals and Greater Desires

Perhaps it's time to stir up our dreams and goals for the future. Desire has been defined as a deep longing, a wish expressed in words. If we think of an idea long enough, we'll begin to talk about it. Speaking aloud empowers what we've been thinking. As we mull over our dreams, we'll find ourselves being drawn toward those possibilities. We can accomplish far more than we ever thought we could accomplish if we line up our desires with those God has for us.

An Assignment

List various aspects of your life on paper under these headings: Physical, Emotional, Intellectual, Educational, Spiritual, Relationships with Friends, and Relationships with Family. Make columns underneath each category. Write under each area what you'd like to accomplish in the next six months. Don't make these plans too lofty but slightly beyond what you're doing at the present. Draw a line under these and then write, "Goals for the next year." Stretch your desires a bit more.

My first goal in writing was to publish a one-page article which was all I could do at that time. I began to polish my writing skills by journaling each day.

You need to continue with projections for the following year, enlarging each phase of your life. For the third year, dream still larger. The norm is to set short-term goals too high and long-term goals too low. The underlying directive is to commit the project to the Lord knowing that He is the secret ingredient of success.

Pull this plan out of the files periodically and read it aloud. Remember, rehearsing what we want in life draws us toward our dreams sometimes with little conscious effort. Ultimately, it's God's call. Our finite minds can make all kinds of elaborate plans, but God has the last word. Human tendency is to settle for what *looks* good, but God holds out for what *is* good. We should never allow our trust in God to fade.

My sister-in-law, Mickey, is past ninety years old and just announced she's ready to begin writing again. She published two books over twenty years ago. She is blind in one eye because of a detached retina, and she doesn't see well out of the other. However, she refuses to give up on her desire to write more books.

Her husband, Don, is ninety-five and still goes to work almost every day to the farm implement business he established just after World War II. He sold it to his son a number of years ago, but Don continues to work there. He knows almost every farmer in his territory and does a lot of PR for their business.

Don also has a hobby of collecting antique implement seats from all over the world. This fulfills a goal to be active in doing something he enjoys. As he adds to his collection, he finds pleasure in discovering a one-of-a-kind seat that may have been in someone's barn for a hundred years or more.

Differences Between Desire and Expectation

Our desires sometimes get tangled with expectations. One day Carey complained, "I hardly accomplished anything I planned today. Phone calls and people dropping by disrupted my day."

"Were you able to help them?"

"Well, yes. Everyone thanked me for my input."

"Perhaps God made your schedule for you today."

"Yeah," he laughed. "You're probably right."

God knows exactly where we are—whether our health and energy are failing or perhaps we simply think it's time to quit. The Lord never expects more than His provision for us to move ahead. Our capabilities, like osteoporosis, may cause the heights of our ambitions to shrink, but they shouldn't completely fade away.

God Whispers Words of Encouragement

Ted came to the retreat center, worn-out and discouraged. He knew his relationship with God had grown weak, and he wondered if it could be restored. He sat on the glider on the porch at the little Casa we'd built down in the woods.

Suddenly, two sparrows flew directly in front of his face. Startled, he was reminded, "What is the price of two sparrows—one copper coin? But not a single sparrow can fall to the ground without your Father knowing it" (Matt. 10:29 NLT). *If God loves even a sparrow, surely He still loves me,* Ted surmised.

Around evening, Ted returned to the porch. Two deer wandered out of the forest to graze in the meadow down the hill. He recalled the verse, "As a deer gets thirsty for streams of water, I truly am thirsty for you, O God" (Ps. 42:1 CEV). He was aware of his growing thirst for God. He grabbed his Bible and began to read—to drink Living Water to revive hope.

It had been some time since he'd read the Bible. And moment by moment, as he read, he felt himself revitalized. He'd searched for God and found Him. This stirred up his desire to grow closer and closer to the Lord.

The next morning, Ted walked out on the hill toward a swing under a vine-covered arbor. I watched him as he turned and began running back toward the house. Breathlessly he said, "I looked up and watched a bald eagle sail over and light at the top of that tall walnut tree. God reminded me—I can still run and not be weary. I can mount up as on wings of eagles. I'm so encouraged. God is fulfilling the desires of my heart. Now I know that I can return home and face my problems with confidence."

Refocus

As we grow older, our desire for material things usually becomes less significant and this is good. Materialism doesn't tempt us as it did in younger years. "But Christ has shown me that what I once thought was valuable is worthless" (Phil. 3:7 CEV).

I have a great desire to bring hope and encouragement to those who age. I'd like to think I could encourage every senior with the fact they can expect God to be at work in their lives until the day He calls them home.

When we line up our desires with the things God has planned for us, we follow under the banner Jesus carries and walk in victory day by day.

> "May he give you the desire of your heart and make all your plans succeed. We will shout for joy when you are victorious and will lift up our banners in the name of our God" (Ps. 20:4–5).

King David had a burning desire to build a temple for the Lord, but God had his son fulfill that dream. We may also have to pass some of our hopes and dreams to the next generation, praying they will pick up the baton and keep on running. Lord, give us the commitment to stir up God-given desires that have been buried beneath the cares of the day.

Keep Shining

The night Carey died, our daughter, Kathy drove me home from the hospital. A huge shooting star blazed across the sky. "Look!" she exclaimed. "Just like Dad, he too went out in a blaze of glory." This can be our greatest desire—to shine ever brighter as we near the end.

LIFE APPLICATION

1. Have you given up on dreams that might still be revived?
2. Are you rusting out, burning out, or just feel like you're wearing out?
3. What has been the most difficult trial in your life?
4. Have you been able to forgive everyone—including yourself?
5. Are you committed to continue walking in forgiveness?
6. Are you willing to follow the assignments in this chapter and set goals for different aspects of your life?
7. Do you continue to reach out in love to those around you?
8. Do you get upset when your plans get interrupted?
9. What is your main focus in life?
10. Do you take notice of the ways God is at work around you?

19
CHECK-OUT TIME

...man goes to his eternal home ...
Ecclesiastes 12:5

As mortals, we live within the confines of time and space. Astronomers have used the Hubble space telescope and found billions of galaxies far beyond the Milky Way. They refer to this discovery as the "known universe." They know there is far more that is unknown.

Since it's impossible for brilliant men to fathom an end to space, why wouldn't they at least consider the possibility of there being no end of time? To accept these mysteries takes faith. It is also by faith we anticipate eternity someday bursting forth into full-blown reality.

Mind-Boggling

Inventors and technologists boggle our minds with what they've accomplished after years of study and trial and error. But all their discoveries will someday be outdated. God spoke only a Word, and the universe and the billions of other miracles burst into existence. It was only in man that He placed a spirit that will never grow old, be outdated, or die.

Our Heavenly Father had plans for us from the beginning—arranging a pit stop for us here on earth before we move on into the outer realm of eternity. He and His Son Jesus have prepared an unimaginable kingdom under the canopy of heaven where He will

154

reign as our King of kings and Lord of lords.

Jesus came to earth to pay our debts so we could live in the heavenly mansion He's preparing. There will be no mortgage, no rent. We'll never receive a utility bill. He is the light and He warms us with His love. We will stay healthy because Jesus is our Bread of Life. Living Water will quench our thirst.

Develop the Fruit of the Spirit

Throughout our lives and before check-out time, we're given opportunities to develop the fruit of the Spirit (Gal. 5:21–22):

It takes *peace* to deal with a tiny infant's constant demand for attention. But the *wonder* of the baby's cooing and laughter make it all worthwhile. During childhood when parents are faced with training a child, it is important to be *gentle* and *kind.* "Don't keep on scolding and nagging your children, making them angry and resentful. Rather, bring them up with the loving discipline the Lord himself approves" (Eph. 6:4 TLB).

Adolescence is a time when young people are hyper-emotional and bent on doing things their own way. Parents need *patience* and *self-control* in handling their swinging moods and outbursts.

During these difficult years, teens may dislike their parents and parents sometimes find it difficult to care much for their teenagers. My husband and I had an agreement that helped us stay together: If either of us left, we had to take all four of our children with us.

Adulthood spans many years of working and achieving. It's a time to hold steady and be *faithful* in dealing with problems with the family and our jobs.

Growing older is a time to polish *goodness* by utilizing all the other fruits of the Spirit to make *love* our crowning virtue.

Our Last Challenge

Eventually, Father Time will crack the door opening into eternity. Some feel the Grim Reaper is lurking nearby. But as God's children, we believe it is a glorious time for us to meet Jesus and be ushered into a far better place.

There, Jesus, as the bridegroom of the church, offers us the wedding ring of commitment—love which will encircle us forever.

When my father was dying, he spoke to me softly. "Sweetheart, there's someone at the door. Let them in." Perhaps it was an angel coming to take him home. God chose this time to welcome him into eternity, a world without end.

God Never Forgets Us

Scripture tells us God has engraved us on the palms of His hand (Isa 49:16 NIV). He holds us tight. All the demons of hell can never pry open His hand to rob, kill, or destroy us now. "I give them eternal life. … My Father, who has given them to me, is greater than all; no one can snatch them out of my Father's hand" (John 10:28–29).

When Does God Heal?

A short time before my husband died, a man from church told him, "I saw you in a vision, totally well and healed." Carey thanked him for his encouraging words, but asked, "Did you see me here or in heaven?" The man stammered, "I don't know." Carey seemed to have known his healing would not come until after he passed from this life.

Prepare to Leave a Legacy

Dean was born with scarcely more than a brain stem. Doctors told his parents he would not live. But Dean clung to life. Though he survived, the doctors said he'd never walk or talk.

But his mom, dad, and brothers were determined to prove the doctors wrong. They worked with Dean for five years before he took his first step. Over time he also learned to say a few words. But by the time he was sixteen, his parents could no longer handle him, so they placed him in a special-needs home. There, he lived until he was eighteen, when he suffered heart failure and died.

His family spoke at his funeral and told what this severely mentally challenged child had taught them. One brother said, "Dean taught me gratitude. He would jump up and down, squealing with delight when I brought him a simple gift—even a stick of gum."

The second brother bit his lip. "He taught me joy as he laughed at a kitten or a fly on the wall."

The third brother choked up. "Dean taught me love. He recognized me. When I came in the door, he'd fall on the floor, hug me around my knees, and say, 'Love, love.'"

Dean's mom said, "His birth and life were the source of another great miracle because I had to turn to God for strength, wisdom, and patience. Dean's example, along with ours, caused a number of our family members to trust God and come to accept Jesus as the Lord of their lives. In spite of Dean's very limited capabilities, he left a powerful legacy."

Regardless of our inadequacies, God gives all of us the ability to leave a legacy. He has a purpose for everything and every single person He created.

We Can Be Confident We'll Make It to the Other Side

As a child we played a game called, "Red Rover, Red Rover." We stood in two lines facing each other, tightly clasping each other's hands. Someone on the opposite side would call out, "Red Rover, Red Rover, let (child's name) come over." The named child would run to the opposite side full force, to try to break through the line. They looked for what they considered to be the weakest link in hopes to break through. In a similar way, Satan spitefully attacks us. He is forever looking for our weakest or most vulnerable spot in an attempt to break our commitment to God.

We stand linked with Jesus, waiting for God to call our name. Jesus runs with us, to make sure we break through all the barriers between us and eternal life. We'll charge full speed ahead with confidence in His driving force.

I'm in the process of laying this world's visa aside. The Lord has completed my heavenly citizenship papers and adopted me as His own. I like to think those who have gone before will be waving and shouting as they await my arrival. I'm learning to speak the language of "love" because that will be the universal language of heaven.

Someday we'll have spacesuits to replace these earth-suits. Unlike the bulky garments of astronauts, our weightless spirits will be wrapped in robes of righteousness.

Moving On

In 2007, we sold the farm with its three houses, barn, and storage shed, all packed with years of accumulation. It was almost with reckless abandon that I got rid of things. Ultimately, I called Good Shepherd Mission who sent three men, a large truck, and trailer and filled them with everything except things I needed to keep. My excess "stuff" could be sold at their resale shop.

A tremendous weight lifted from my shoulders as I watched them drive out the gate with former "treasures." In somewhat the same way, it will even be a greater relief when we can leave the excess baggage of this world behind.

Peaceful Departure

When the time comes for us to lay everything down, I'd like to think we will be ready to leave as peacefully as the sun begins to set and daylight fades away. I pray that we will approach death with the same perspective as William Cullen Bryant did in his poem, *Thanatopsis:* "We go with an unfaltering faith, to lie down to pleasant dreams."

Take Off Time

Time passes quickly. Soon the conductor will cry out, "All aboard," announcing it is time to leave. In one sense, it seems our life on earth has been short, but we now discover it's almost over. We've been compared to fog or a wisp of smoke, quickly burned away or carried away by a puff of wind.

We're no longer so focused on growing older, but on growing upward. We determine to face each day with great expectancy

> "because of the tender mercy of our God, by which the rising sun will come to us from heaven to shine on those living in darkness and in the shadow of death, to guide our feet into the path of peace" (Luke 1:78–79).

As the last gift of our going-away party is unwrapped, we can put away our toys and haul the rest to Goodwill, hoping they will brighten someone else's day. Whether it's a Rolex or a Timex—neither will be needed any more.

I think I hear someone singing, "Get on board, little children. There's room for many more." Won't you come along?

Life Application

1. Is it difficult for you to think outside the realms of time and space?
2. In what ways has your patience been tested?
3. Are you convinced that prayer and love are two of the most powerful forces in the universe?
4. Has there been a time in your life when you had to work to be long-suffering?
5. Are you still struggling with why some things happen in this world?
6. Do you believe God will perfect all things in eternity?
7. When difficulties show up in your life, do you become bitter or better?
8. Do you live your life in such a way that you would be content for God to call you home any time?
9. Are you aware of how you are to grow the fruit of the Spirit in your life?
10. What lessons have you learned during each stage of your life?

20

GRIEVING OUR LOSSES

...and mourners go about the streets.
Ecclesiastes 12:5

Tears wash over our souls—a God-given provision that releases a portion of our grief. They're a part of the healing process when we deal with a broken heart. However, God would not have us set up camp and live in a state of sadness. Jesus stands nearby, to help us bear our burdens.

> "The Spirit of the Sovereign LORD is on me. ... He has sent me to bind up the brokenhearted, to proclaim freedom for the captives and release from darkness for the prisoners, ... to comfort all who mourn, and provide for those who grieve in Zion—to bestow on them a crown of beauty instead of ashes, the oil of gladness instead of mourning, and a garment of praise instead of a spirit of despair" (Isa. 61:1–3).

David Prayed for His Baby Boy

David fasted and pled with God to heal his infant son, born to Bathsheba. He lay prostrate before the Lord. When the child died, his servants wouldn't go near him because they were afraid of his reaction. When David saw they were avoiding him, he asked if the child had died. They told him the truth. To their surprise, he got up, washed, and ate. His attendants were confused about his response, but he told them that as long as his child lived, he had hope—but now there was nothing he could do. In his sorrow, he explained, "I can't bring him back! Someday I will join him in death, but he can't return to me" (2 Sam. 12:23 CEV).

David refused to stay stuck in the pit of despair. In his grief, he accepted the final verdict—his baby was dead. Later, he wrote that we may weep in our beds at night, but in the morning we're to look for joy. Solomon added his bit of wisdom when he wrote that there are windows of time when it is appropriate to express all kinds of emotions—weeping, laughing, mourning, and dancing. All these emotions are God-given gifts for us to live life to the fullest.

People are prone to think their circumstances are worse than others. When I worked as the Director of Spiritual Affairs in a psychiatric hospital, I visited with a woman who was grieving over the death of her husband. I explained I was sorry, as I had also lost my husband. She turned to me and wailed, "But mine's not coming back."

Words are Inadequate in Expressing Deep Emotions

We cannot express our deepest emotions in words. In the depths of our grief, we cry or weep. When we're extremely happy, we shout and laugh. In the midst of pain, we may moan or groan. We show excitement when we jump up and down and clap our hands. And nothing conveys more contentment than a cooing baby.

We usually stumble verbally in awkward situations. Actions sometimes come across with a more powerful message. We show compassion with touch and hugs. Deep feelings echoing from our hearts are expressed in ways other than words.

Our Darkest Hour

Our oldest son, Rick, fell into the depths of depression to the point he became overwhelmed. On a couple of occasions, he briefly mentioned his struggle, but we didn't realize the seriousness of his despair. We had no idea of the magnitude of his battle … until that terrible day when he took his life. After his death, we discovered poems he'd written that reflected some of the pain he experienced. This is a brief portion from one of them:

> These days that last forever
> Don't last long in eternity
> I think I would feel better
> If only time would set me free.

Even with the excruciating pain of the loss of our son, there were lessons we needed to learn. The Scripture I'd asked them to use at his funeral was a continuing reminder to reach out to others. "He comforts us when we are in trouble so we can share that same comfort with others in trouble" (2 Cor. 1:4 CEV).

Shortly after this horrific loss, I attended a retreat in Galveston. Our speaker asked us not to say anything the next morning until we met for a devotional. She suggested we take a walk to see if God would speak to us in some way we could share with the group. I walked barefoot along the beach, dragging my feet in the sand, burdened with a grief that weighed heavy on my heart. I stood watching the tide roll in. The Lord must have been nearby as he sent small waves of peace. I marveled, "Lord, it was such a miracle that You walked on the water." A thought washed over my mind: *Is it any less a miracle that you walk through deep water and are not overcome?*

Emotional healing came slowly, but it was as great as any miracle of physical healing. Months later, I ran across the full Scripture I'd heard a portion of that day on the beach. I didn't remember ever reading it before. "When you pass through the waters, I will be with you; and when you pass through the rivers, they will not sweep over you. When you walk through the fire, you will not be burned; the flames will not set you ablaze. For I am the LORD your God, the Holy One of Israel, your Savior" (Isa. 43:2–3 NIV). In a precious and personal way, the Lord assured me He would walk with me through my pain. *Thank You, loving Father.*

The earthquakes that shake our emotional world are often followed by multiple after-shocks. My psychologist husband's first reaction to our son Rick's death was, "I'm quitting counseling. If I missed it with my own son, how could I ever expect to help anyone else?"

Disbelieving, I stared at him. "Carey, that's exactly what Satan would have you do. He not only wanted to destroy Rick's life, he wants to destroy the effectiveness of the rest of our lives also." Satan designs his devious and evil schemes to cause as wide a range of devastation as possible. *Get out of my face, you conniving enemy!*

Carey picked up his briefcase and headed back to the office. He continued to counsel and reach out to others with a message of hope. We refused to allow Satan to destroy us with his wicked schemes. The Holy Spirit comforted us and helped us walk through the darkest period of our lives. We didn't know what to do, but we made the decision to not give up. We slowly moved ahead by reaching out to others who were hurting. As we touched the lives of others, God comforted us.

Time and again when I felt I was drowning in despair, I knew the one who walked on the water would lift me up. When the waters are rough and deep, I'm confident He will not let me sink. When I find myself between a rock and a hard place, I'll climb up on that Rock for safety. By my Abba Father's grace, the hard places in life will not crush me.

Encouragement from Others

After Rick's death, we received many heartwarming notes from loved ones. One friend wrote she'd just moved into a new home and went in the bathroom. The emptiness was an echo of loneliness. Her heart ached as she thought, "This is how Carey and Louise feel."

Without consciously thinking of the emptiness, she began to hang curtains, towels, and pictures. She placed knick-knacks about the room. The next morning when she walked in the room, the sun was streaming through the bathroom window. The entire room was warm and inviting. It was if God whispered, "I will once again shine in Louise and Carey's lives."

The Necessity of Forgiveness

In spite of the comfort of God and others, the devastating blow of our son's death was heartrending. As I wrestled with the gut-wrenching tragedy, I realized most of life's hardest struggles must be met head-on with forgiveness.

When dealing with trauma, it's not unusual for instant replays to come tromping back in to haunt us. Satan surely must have instigated the instant replay, complete with three-dimensional visuals, surround-sound enhancement, smells, and even vivid color.

There's some truth in the saying, "Beside every grave, there are those who look for someone or someplace to lay the blame." I started thinking of times I didn't act in Rick's best interest because I was too preoccupied with my own problems in life. There were times when I didn't show him the love and support he deserved and needed. This caused me to place a huge bag of guilt on my shoulders.

Next, I put a chunk of blame on Carey's tray because he was an absent father. He hadn't taken his son under his wing and worked with him.

I filled other buckets of blame and dumped them on Rick's wife, while other platters were served to his friends who didn't return his calls when he phoned to tell them he needed to talk. I wrote down the reasons I felt I was justified in my unforgiveness.

It dawned on me how ungodly it was to be unforgiving. So I laid my list aside my list and prayed the Lord would walk me through the steps of forgiveness. Not unlike peeling the layers of an onion, each person I forgave brought tears when I took off those layers of resentment.

It was an ongoing process of forgiving myself and others. God reminded me that Jesus' sacrifice *was* more than enough to cover every sin of commission and omission.

It was sobering when almost six months after his death, Rick appeared to me in a dream one night and said, "Mom, please let me go."

I thought I'd forgiven everyone involved until Carey and I attended a conference in Nashville—a full two years after Rick's death. On the final night of the conference, the speaker's lesson was on forgiveness. I kept thinking of Rick's death. *Why, Lord? I think I've forgiven every person involved.*

Deep in my spirit, I felt the Lord confront me. "You've not forgiven Me."

I sat in shock. *What is this all about?*

After that message, we went to the pastor's home to spend the night. The thought of forgiving God troubled me. Was it possible I *did* hold unforgiveness toward God?

When the others were ready for bed that night, they asked if I planned to stay up. I replied, "Yes, I have some business with God that needs my attention."

Alone in the parlor, I pulled out my notepad and pen. I began to journal, and as I did, defensive thoughts rose to the forefront of my mind. *Lord, why do You say I haven't forgiven You? You've never done anything wrong—nothing that needs forgiveness.*

The Lord nudged me. "True, but in the recesses of your mind, you blamed Me for failing to intervene when Rick made the final preparations to take his life."

I caught my breath as I recalled times when I'd been upset because God didn't do something in those last moments. I laid down my pen and thought of the accusations I'd made. *Lord, why didn't You prompt someone to call him on the phone, even if it had been a wrong number? You could have had someone knock at the door or You could have even caused an earthquake. Merciful God, why didn't You do something?* I shuddered, convicted of blaming the Lord. My heart squeezed tears up into my eyes until they overflowed their banks. These tears contained a mixture of shame and pain, leaking from cracks in my broken heart.

Cautiously, I picked up my pen again and began to write slowly. "Lord, forgive me for blaming You for not intervening." I paused at the impact of my next thought, but deliberately wrote, "Tonight I forgive You for letting my son die." Tears streamed down my face as I confessed this pent-up accusation.

Within moments, the Lord spoke ever so tenderly, "And I forgive you for letting my Son die." I wept with a deep realization. I *was* guilty. My sins most certainly played a part in nailing Jesus to the cross. Almost immediately, God wrapped a blanket of comfort around my trembling shoulders that had grown cold from this chilling blame.

A heavy load lifted from my shoulders that night. There will always be a jagged scar in my heart, but it is no longer so raw and sensitive. God touched the untouchable.

Shortly after Rick's death, I wondered if there'd ever be more than five minutes when I didn't think of him. I struggled to resist the devil's assaults. He was relentless with his blame and guilt for a while, but when I continued to resist him, he slowly pulled back from his dastardly attack and eventually slithered away.

Forgiveness is Hard

Forgiveness plays a major role getting past trauma or hurts from the past. It frequently involves forgiving ourselves, others, and yes, even God. I realized that when I blame circumstances, it is as if I'm blaming God for allowing those things to happen.

Though the steps of forgiveness are painful, they are essential in the process of healing wounded emotions.

Different Reasons for Tears

One form of tears comes from regret. We could easily spend an inordinate amount of time moaning and groaning over the ways we should have done things different in life. As we grow older, the list may grow longer. Thank God, He gives us hope.

"You'll forget your troubles; they'll be like old, faded

photographs. Your world will be washed in sunshine, every shadow dispersed by dayspring. Full of hope, you'll relax, confident again" (Job 11:16–18 MSG).

How blessed we are that our Heavenly Father wants to set us free from guilt and shame.

Tears can be a sign of letting go. There may be times when we need to turn loose of some of our hopes and dreams. We may need to turn our loved ones over to God, after finding we aren't able to make them change their lives.

Some weep out of self-pity, or the "poor me" syndrome. I could hardly keep from chuckling when an older friend of mine would introduce herself with a whiney, "I'm just a pore, little ole widder woman."

She must have kept a record of all the dismal things that happened, so she could tell every pitiful detail to all her friends and relatives. For instance, one day when we were visiting, she bemoaned the fact that Runnels County, where she lived, had more cancer patients per capita than any other county in the state. After we left her house that day, our son Paul remarked, "Just think. They could build a huge billboard in front of the courthouse with bold letters, Runnels County, Cancer Capital of Texas."

Some choose to be mournful. Jill, a friend in Idaho, went to nursing homes and houses of shut-ins to sing and play her keyboard. She reached out to cheer people by playing their favorite songs. Every time she visited one older woman, Jill would ask her what she wanted her to play. The woman would respond mournfully, "Play anything you like, dearie, just as long as it's sad."

I smile when I remember attending a wedding, where the groom's mother walked down the aisle of the church, with a huge box of tissue tucked under her arm. It looked like she was announcing loud and clear how she hated to see her only child get married and move on with his life. I must remember however, some tears at weddings are anticipated. When our daughter was married in an outdoor courtyard, Carey lamented, "It was so hot that day, my eyes started sweating."

Some tears are shed in anticipation. When a loved one is seriously ill and the doctor has forewarned they're going to die, tears come early. My husband's physician told me two years before Carey died, "He'll not survive the cancer; it has metastasized all over his body." I did most of my crying before his life ended. I worked through many aspects of grief, so that when the time came, it was almost a relief to know he'd finally been set free from suffering.

There are tears of manipulation and even tears of joy, but I believe the God-given purpose of tears is as an expression of sorrow distilled by His mercy. They are a part of the healing process for those who are hurting.

Reluctantly, we offer the Lord our broken hearts for Him to mend. On our own, we have no idea where all the pieces belong.

No Tears in Heaven

Scripture tells us, God collects our tears in a bottle. This puzzled me. Why would God keep our tears? Perhaps there will be an angel standing outside the pearly gates, ready to hand back our own bottle of tears. Perhaps he'll ask us to pour them out with the blessed assurance, "There will be no more tears."

There is a huge mural in Carthage, Missouri, where Samuel J. Butcher, the artist of *Precious Moments,* painted a picture of heaven with many small angels rejoicing in resplendent glory. At the pearly gates, a little cherub stands to hand out tissues to those about to enter and points to a sign nearby which reads, "No tears in heaven." Our compassionate Heavenly Father promises to remove all our sorrows.

> "They're his people, he's their God. He'll wipe every
> tear from their eyes. Death is gone for good—tears gone,
> crying gone, pain gone" (Rev. 21:3–4 MSG).

The Valley of Bacca

In Scripture there is a Valley named Bacca. It was known as the valley of weeping. Later in Scripture it was referred to as a place of springs.

In the same way, we may find ourselves in a place of weeping, but we can look up with the hope that springs of Living Water will someday flow from that place.

Carey's Departure

Carey shared an amazing story with me a couple of nights before he died. "I felt the Lord held me in his arms all night." He believed God gave him a glimpse of His throne room. I was astonished, but for some reason, I didn't think to ask him what it looked like!

A few days before his death, I reminded him: "For our twenty-fifth anniversary, we went to Hawaii. On our thirtieth, we went to Israel." My voice faltered, "You kept asking me where I wanted to go on this, our thirty-fifth anniversary and I never could make up my mind. Now it looks like you're going without me."

LIFE APPLICATION

1. Should people be ashamed to cry?
2. Should a person limit the length of time they spend in grieving?
3. How do you express your deepest emotions such as grief, joy, and pain?
4. Have you dealt with all aspects of forgiveness following your darkest hours?
5. Is there anything for which you need to forgive God?
6. How do you show compassion to hurting people?
7. Do you ever cry tears of self-pity?
8. Can you accept God's forgiveness and not keep living with tears of regret?
9. Do you know people who use tears as manipulation?
10. Explain how tears can be beneficial in the grieving process.

21
THE MAP TO FIND THE TREASUSRE

Remember him—before the silver cord is severed.
Ecclesiastes 12:6

When an old-timey clock winds down, the ticking stops. One day the message from the brain in this old-time body will fail to trigger a heartbeat. Listen as you might, the thumping of the heart will grow silent. The life blood coursing through veins becomes stagnant— a sure sign that the life of man or beast has shut down.

The umbilical cord severed at birth is the signal for an infant to survive outside the womb. In a similar way, when the silver cord is severed, the spirit is released to live outside this earthly body. The connection that tethered the spirit to the body will be snipped. In God's scheme of things, the beautiful spirit-being inside will be free to soar.

There is a correlation in scripture between planting seed and the process of dying. In plant life, a seed is buried in the ground and the outer shell breaks to allow the embryo to spring to life. If this doesn't happen, the seed remains dormant—a single seed.

Our spirit is trapped inside this shell of flesh. At death, when the silver cord is severed, the spirit becomes far more than it has ever been. Like cutting the ribbon to celebrate a grand opening, the severed cord is snipped to open to a new life.

An Uncommon Fraction

I had a mental block when I heard the word "math" in school. The only reason I took extra math courses was because my boyfriend, a whiz at math, volunteered to help me with my homework. My puppy love for him faded, and I never learned to like math.

In spite of this dislike, my son, Paul, had a concept about a mathematical fraction that intrigued me. He suggested we let a fraction illustrate our priorities. The top number of the fraction would represent treasures we lay up in heaven. The number grows larger when we put God first and offer Him our first fruits. The top number grows larger when we draw near to God and we become more like Jesus. Most of the things above the line would represent our love for God and our fellowman.

The line between the top number (the numerator) and the bottom number (the denominator) might represent the silver cord Solomon spoke about in Ecclesiastes. For this illustration, it separates heavenly riches from worldly assets.

The bottom number would represent our focus on things of this world. That number grows larger when we place emphasis on self—me, my, and mine. It grows larger when we pamper ourselves by seeking more money, power, and prestige.

In school, we were taught if the numerator became larger than the denominator, the fraction would be labeled as *uncommon* because its value would be more than a whole. When our focus is to lay up treasures in heaven, it is evident we consider them to be more important than earthly possessions. This makes us uncommon. We're different from the everyday man on the street.

When the silver cord is severed, our soul is set free to be reunited with the spiritual treasures we've sent on ahead.

The richest man on earth can't buy a home in heaven. The greatest celebrity may not be known by God. A string of initials following my name doesn't mean I have godly wisdom. All those things hanging below the silver cord will drop away at death. Many of the things the world counts as so important will come crashing down—insignificant in God's sight.

Wealth is Often Temporary

An acquaintance was worth ten million dollars. One day he boasted, "Someday I intend to be worth a hundred million dollars."

I looked at him in disbelief and asked, "What then?"

He stared at me as if I'd asked a stupid question. A few months later, he was charged with mail fraud and sentenced to two years in federal prison. The government seized all his assets.

After he was released from prison, he was not only financially broke—he came out as a broken and humbled man.

His wife said the experience was worth every penny they lost because her husband was stripped of his prideful attitude.

> "Don't love the world's ways. Don't love the world's goods. Love of the world squeezes out love for the Father. Practically everything that goes on in the world—wanting your own way, wanting everything for yourself, wanting to appear important—has nothing to do with the Father. It just isolates you from Him. The world in all its wanting, wanting, is on its way out—but whoever does what God wants is set for eternity" (1 John 2:15–17 MSG).

Wrong Emphasis

In the little town where I was raised, there was a ne'er-do-well man who bragged that one day he would be very wealthy because he'd been named as the sole heir of his aunt's estate.

Year after year, he waited. His aging aunt went into a nursing home that ate up most of her assets. When the aunt eventually died, there was only enough money left for her nephew to buy a small house on the wrong side of the tracks. He wasn't even able to enjoy the pitiful amount he received because he was met with an untimely death.

What is of Real Value?

When my husband and I lived in Denver, we kept girls who were on probation from juvenile court. One girl's mother came by regularly to bring her gifts. One day she brought her a purse and left quickly to go on her way.

Her daughter threw the gift across the room and shouted, "Why can't she understand I don't want her stinking gifts. I just want her to act like she cares enough to spend time with me."

A gift without love is like paying your taxes—we pay them, but don't enjoy it. The truth is, we can give without loving but we can't love without giving,

Attitudes about Losses

When I sold our farm in 2007, I made a mistake of allowing my broker to invest most of my money in the stock market. At my age, this was not wise. In 2008 I watched the Dow Jones fall day after day, until one day I called my broker. "I'm bleeding to death, help me." I showed poor judgment again by encouraging him to sell my stocks when the market was near the bottom.

I was distraught and started thinking of places I could cut corners. I could cut back on giving to the church and other charitable organizations. All at once I realized Satan had prepared a trap of fear and I'd fallen headlong into it. *Oh no you don't, you conniver.* In defiance, I increased my monthly support of one missionary and contributed a sizable amount to another.

A sense of peace flowed over me as I determined, *I will not be intimidated by the devil and all his whisperings about my going broke. Satan wants me to focus on the loss of money rather than trusting God.* My Heavenly Father is my Jehovah Jireh—not my material possessions. When I accepted that God would take care of me, I began sleeping at night without tossing, turning, and kicking myself for being an unwise steward.

Wise Stewards

George Pepperdine, who founded the Western Auto Stores, also helped establish the beautiful university in California that bears his name and overlooks Malibu Beach. At one point, when he was struggling in a financial crisis, someone asked if he didn't regret giving away so much money. "No," he replied. "My faith is my fortune." I believe God smiles on those who freely give and refuse to look back.

We're encouraged to be wise stewards, regardless of how little we've accumulated. Possessions aren't wrong or even unimportant, but we are to be wise in the way we use our money. We can enjoy this world's goods, yet refuse to become overly attached to them. God watches how trustworthy we are with our worldly possessions to decide how we will handle heavenly treasures. It's reassuring to know we can't out-give God. We don't give to get, but there's a godly principle that as we take care of others, the Lord takes care of us.

Refiner's Fire

In Africa, we visited a refinery where they were purifying gold. The caldrons were heated until the impurities floated to the top and were skimmed off. In the same way, when the heat in our lives gets turned up by hot and sticky situations, impure thoughts and attitudes tend to float to the surface. Genuine faith helps us endure fiery trials and we ask God to skim off our impurities.

Perhaps in eternity, we'll look back at our time on earth and see how God orchestrated the refining process. We pray we'll be patient as He puts the finishing touches on us.

Little Things Can Be of Great Value

Shortly before my dad died, he apologized because he didn't have many assets to leave his eight children. My brother corrected him.

"Dad, you made sure we all got a college education. And the life you and Mom lived is a legacy that is worth far more than *any* amount of money."

It is difficult to understand how seemingly small and insignificant things matter to God. Jesus gave the example of the widow's two mites and said her gift was worth more than all the rest. We'll possibly spend the first thousand years in heaven slapping our foreheads, saying, "I didn't realize how much little things would count."

My dad was in a serious accident and burned so extensively he wasn't expected to live. My brother sneaked his four-year-old son into the hospital so he could see his beloved granddad. Dad gasped for air as he greeted them. My nephew, Mark, spoke softly, "Granddad, I brought you something," and placed a nickel in his granddad's hand. Dad had tears in his eyes as he whispered, "Thank you, son. I'm going to put this in a special place and never spend it." He valued this little gift because it was wrapped in a precious package of love.

Surprises and Rewards

It is sheer joy to surprise someone with a gift they have longed for. Though we were a poor family, my older sister suggested Dad buy Mom a watch for Christmas one year. He gave Sis some money and asked her to go pick one out.

Early on Christmas morning, Mother opened the small package. She literally jumped up and down and ran over to hug Dad's neck and thank him. "I never thought I'd have a watch of my very own." I wonder—does it excite God as He prepares priceless surprises for His children?

The greatest blessing we will ever receive will be to hear God say, "Excellent! You are a good servant. Since I can trust you with small things, I will let you rule over ten of my cities" (Luke 19:17 NCV). In this statement, I believe God not only refers to worldly goods but the way we have used our talents, time, and efforts day after day.

A Christian's Identity

Our identity as Christians should be so unique that others will seek us out to see if they can find the same treasures we found. We'll not only be uncommon among men, but extraordinary in the sight of God. It takes courage to be different—to be willing to be a peculiar people led by God's unseen Spirit. We learn to say NO to instant gratification and be willing to wait in anticipation for what we will receive in eternity.

There will come a time when our shelf life will expire and our year-model will be outdated. Replacement parts are unavailable. Our faith-based works will be on display as to what we considered to be of true significance in our lives.

All the glittering seductions of this life will pale in the light of the true wealth of eternity. The beautiful spirit inside is unseen now, but it will someday overshadow any package we've been wrapped in here. Where we spend our time, money and effort is a clear indication of what we hold dear. Our lives are richly enhanced by Christ living in us as our hope of glory.

Times here may be rough for a while, but I love Dr. Tony Campolo's sermon about the crucifixion and the resurrection of Jesus. He repeatedly shouted, "It's Friday, but Sunday's coming!"

LIFE APPLICATION

1. Have you considered what it will be like when the spirit is separated from the body?
2. Can you compare the body to a seed—and brokenness as an indication you are fully submitted to God?
3. Do you trust God to be your true provider?
4. How are you investing in eternal things?
5. What does it mean to be a wise steward?
6. Is it wrong to have great wealth? Explain. What are the dangers?
7. When you are generous, how does it make you feel?
8. Have you ever surprised someone with something you knew they wanted?
9. Do you spend too much time thinking about material possessions?
10. In this chapter, a Christian was described as an uncommon fraction. What does that mean to you?

22

MY MIND KEEPS LOSING FILES

... the golden bowl is broken ...
Ecclesiastes 12:6

S ome Bible scholars believe the golden bowl Solomon referred to in Ecclesiastes refers to the brain. Though our minds have served us well over the years, bombarding attacks have left their toll. Not all the circuits work properly, and connections fail to fire up as they once did.

Though the "golden bowl" may not be broken, mine appears to be cracked because input keeps leaking out. It doesn't encourage me when my forgetter works overtime.

However, since scripture says we can renew our mind, God will surely help us stay centered on Him. "Do not conform to the pattern of this world, but be transformed by the renewing of your mind" (Rom. 12:2).

The Use of Our Senses

The things we see, hear, touch, taste, and smell are resources that reinforce memories. It helps to use as many senses as possible to lock things we need to remember in place. For instance, when we want to memorize Scripture, we first look at it in print, read it aloud to hear it, and involve touch by running our finger under the words. Philippians 4:8 emphasizes how we are to think: whatsoever things are lovely, whatsoever things are of good report; if there be any virtue, and if there be any praise, think on these things" (KJV).

Since stress and anxiety make it difficult to think clearly, we can use our five senses to help us relax.

What We See

A magnificent sunrise or sunset brings a peace that settles over our minds. God created gorgeous scenes for our enjoyment.

> "Instead of looking at the fashions, walk out into the fields and look at the wildflowers. They never primp or shop, but have you ever seen color and design quite like it?" (Matt. 6:28–29 MSG).

What We Hear

What we listen to plays a part in renewing the mind. "I'm absorbed in pondering your wise counsel. Yes, your sayings on life are what give me delight" (Ps. 119:23–24 MSG). The word "gospel" literally means good news. God's Word has the ability to bring us hope.

Read encouraging scriptures aloud. Using a confident tone of voice makes it more effective.

Self-talk is extremely important. I'm told we're more likely to believe what we tell ourselves than what someone else tells us. Our words are powerful. "The tongue has the power of life and death" (Prov. 18:21). Don't say negative things about yourself like: "I'm stupid" or "I can't do anything right."

If possible, distance yourself from those who pollute the air with negativity, insults, crude remarks, and profanity.

We are told, "If you have ears, listen to what the Spirit says to the churches" (Rev. 2:17 CEV).

Music is a great spirit-lifter. It is easier to remember the words of a song than a quotation. Music, whether instrumental or vocal, carries a strong message. It is easier to feel God's presence when we're in the midst of praise and worship. Scripture encourages us to speak "to one another with psalms, hymns, and songs from the Spirit. Sing and make music from your heart to the Lord" (Eph. 5:19 NIV).

People have been healed physically and emotionally by listening to hymns and contemporary worship songs. Music not only helps renew our minds—it restores our faith.

What We Taste

Eating and tasting can be used as a metaphor. After a bad experience we're likely to say, "That left a bad taste in my mouth." When we're worried, we might say, "That situation is eating my lunch." If we're angry, we may grumble, "He needs to get a taste of his own medicine." Scripture tells us: "Taste and see that the LORD is good" (Ps. 34:8).

There are foods called "comfort foods." The flavonoids in dark chocolate tend to perk us up. Pizza, ice cream, and potato chips rank high on the list of comfort foods. These foods satisfy our taste buds. We are told, we are what we eat.

It is important to eat healthy foods. Food may either drag us down or perk us up. What we eat affects how we think and feel. Sweets initially energize us, but later they let us down. Some nutritionists say sugar dulls the mind.

What We Touch

The ways we are touched influences our emotions and our thinking. Touch is both physical and emotional. Think of how you think and feel after a pat on the shoulder, a touch on the arm, or a hug. Any of these can play a part in restoring our peace and confidence. A warm touch serves as a wake-up call to our brains to release good hormones that actually keep us healthier. The following story is a great example of how hearing and touch more than likely saved critically ill infants.

My son, Paul, worked as the clinic doctor in a nearby university.

A minister visited him there one day and told him about his daughter who had given birth to premature twins. She called him from the hospital, weeping. "If you want to see your granddaughters alive, come right away. The pediatrician doesn't expect either of them to live."

When the grandfather arrived, he got permission to go into the nursery and place his hands on the tiny babies inside the incubators. There, he began to massage the babies, pat them, and encourage them with soothing words. "Jesus can make you live," he told them. He sang to them, and the nurses were amazed as the babies began to respond by moving and breathing better. The pediatrician encouraged the grandfather to continue to rub their little bodies and talk to them. After the babies rallied, he went home to rest.

He had scarcely fallen asleep when the hospital called again. The babies were slipping away. He dressed quickly and hurried back to the hospital to resume his routine. The pediatrician brought in a recorder so the nurses could record his prayers and songs. When the grandfather grew tired and went home the second time, the pediatrician had the nurses play the recording and take turns massaging the babies. Remarkably, the babies not only survived, they thrived.

Five years later, the pediatrician called the pastor. First, he asked how the twins were doing. After he got a good report, he said, "The real reason I called is to let you know, I have no way of knowing how many babies your recording has saved. Every time we have a baby in crisis, we replay the recording and I have the nurses rub and pat the infants." The combination of touch and hearing played a part in the infants' survival.

What We Smell

Pleasant aromas help us relax. The smell of lavender is said to be soothing. Our prayers are referred to as a sweet smell rising to the throne room of God.

"As far as God is concerned there is a sweet, wholesome fragrance in our lives. It is the fragrance of Christ within us, an aroma to both the saved and the unsaved all around us" (2 Cor. 2:15 TLB).

Enemies of Our Thoughts

Since we live in a world of anger, sarcasm, and criticism, we must keep away from negative conversations.

"We are not fighting against humans. We are fighting against forces and authorities and against rulers of darkness and powers in the spiritual world" (Eph. 6:12 CEV).

The mind is the enemy's favorite battleground. Bad emotions cause the brain to release chemicals that affect our physical, emotional, and spiritual well-being. Smidgens of Satan's lies attach themselves to bits of truth in our thoughts. They're like pesky barnacles—and all too often, we allow them to stick.

Anxiety affects our memory and our thought processes, resulting in confusion and making it difficult to think clearly. One day when I was stressed out, someone asked me to repeat what I'd just said. "Oh, I don't know. I wasn't listening either," I replied. Some refer to small lapses of memory as "senior moments." I'm afraid mine, like an irregular heartbeat, skips on a regular basis.

When we rehearse unpleasant thoughts, it's like carrying a trash bag filled with old garbage. If not removed or taken captive, they link with other rotten thinking. We pray for God to haul all unhealthy memories out and dump them. We'll know the garbage is gone when those thoughts fail to return when we have a brief period of quietness. We shake our shoulders, hold up our heads, and move on.

Aging is a time when the enemy would fill our minds with discouragement. Malfunctioning parts of our bodies are prime targets for Satan's potshots with his flaming arrows in an effort to discourage us. He taunts us with things like "You're not good for anything anymore, and things are going to get worse. And what will you do when you can't take care of yourself?" We must learn to respond by using a powerful Scripture: "I can do all things through Christ, because he gives me strength" (Phil. 4:13 NCV). This tends to smother his fiery darts.

Pray for Wisdom

As I age, I continue to repeat, "Father, today give me the mind of Christ. Let me think godly thoughts. Renew my mind to the sharp status of bygone days. Give me wisdom to know how to live today in a productive way. You are not a God of fear, but that of a sound mind." I pray these Scriptures daily as a protection against dementia. (It seems to be working!)

Taking bad thoughts captive is a lifelong process. It requires ongoing effort to capture those little boogers before they, like chiggers, work their way under our skin and pester the daylights out of us.

Intelligence

Growing older doesn't mean we're unable to learn new things. It does take more effort, but our minds can be challenged to wake up sleepy areas of our brain. Our world grows larger when we pursue new activities and are more involved in others' lives. When we pray for wisdom, we open our hearts to receive input from the Holy Spirit.

Controlling our thought-life makes our minds and bodies not only feel better, but we actually become smarter. Science has proven that even a brain damaged by years of toxic, negative thinking can begin to recover in a matter of days. God constructed our brains in such a way that our minds can be renewed. It is incredibly encouraging to know "we have the mind of Christ" (1 Cor. 2:16).

Humor and Intelligence

Humor gives us more flexibility in our thought-life, as if the brain jumps and whirls with joy. Ideas come quicker, and we access other good thoughts when we're happy. When people brainstorm and laugh together at some outrageous suggestions, they get excited over possibilities and the often come up with innovative ideas.

Fun motivates us. It is inexpensive, enjoyable, and effective. It smashes toxic thoughts. Thoughts of adventure play a vital role in maintaining health and energy. We can be drooping and dragging when a friend calls to suggest we join them for an enjoyable outing. Typically, the immediate response is to feel energized and motivated as we look forward to fun and relaxation.

Laughter has been shown to increase the ability to fight against respiratory infections.

The good news is, if our thoughts are powerful enough to make us sick, they are powerful enough to make us well. Our thoughts lift us up or take us down.

We can always think of excuses for not getting out and taking part in enjoyable activities. "Those who wait for perfect weather will never plant seeds; those who look at every cloud will never harvest crops" (Eccl. 11:4 NCV).

Refuse to accept that the "golden bowl is broken.'" Get up and get out. Laugh a lot, live a lot, and love a lot. God is our free, preventive health insurance. Let this be a time to open up your brain for the Lord to come in and glue the golden bowl back together. Our Savior carefully mends those things that are broken, using His love as the superglue that never fails. "God's Son was before all else, and *by him everything is held together*" (Col. 1:17 CEV, italics mine).

Our minds are extremely powerful and can guarantee us an overcoming walk with the Lord. We ask the Father to renew our minds until they are held together by a solid commitment to concentrate on thoughts that are in sync with His plans for our lives.

LIFE APPLICATION

1. Do you any negative thought patterns that might affect your health?
2. Are you aware that your main battles are not against people or circumstances?
3. Do you find it is difficult to think clearly when you're anxious?
4. Have you learned to pray about what may seem like insignificant situations?
5. How can you learn to take your thoughts captive?
6. It is possible that you have any buried negative emotions?
7. Do you allow any of your problems to be a part of your identity?
8. Can you think of a new thing you'd like to learn?
9. If you live alone, are there ways you can fulfill the need to touch and be touch? (Grandchildren are wonderful for this!)
10. Do you realize what a powerful influence your mind has over your physical, emotional, and spiritual wellbeing?

23
LEAKY FAUCETS

... the pitcher is shattered at the spring ...
Ecclesiastes 12:6

Uh oh. Could Solomon possibly be bringing up the sensitive aging condition with which I'm all too familiar? A pitcher is designed to hold water, right? In our physical body, the only thing comparable is a part of our plumbing system, or more explicitly, the bladder. Sadly, as a person begins to age, this organ may no longer function as it was designed. The container may not be shattered, but it's so worn out, it leaks.

Embarrassing Predicament

In his mid-nineties, my brother called me on the phone. With seemingly no sign of self-consciousness, he said in a matter-of-fact way, "I have to wear diapers now." Because by nature he was dignified and proper, I've always thought of him as a little general. It pleased me to find he continues to retain his sense of dignity in spite of this problem.

My sister, Ruth, my sister-in-law, Flo, and I went for an evening stroll. Flo stepped in a hole and staggered as if she were drunk. We all giggled and Ruth burst out, "Look!" The three of us were standing in the middle of the street with our legs crossed. There was no need to explain. We pointed to one another and burst into peals of laughter.

I wracked my brain. Could anything purposeful come from this curse which assaults many of us traveling these last miles? No amount of wealth, prestige, or power can exempt a person, and Satan delights in humiliating us through our worn-out bodies.

Some Things We Have to Get Over

My friend Sherry shared this experience. "Last night I had the most embarrassing situation ever—it was awful! I went out to eat with my family. Suddenly, I had to go to the bathroom. I hurried but I didn't make it. I was mortified. I cowered in the bathroom. After a time, my daughter sent her two girls to check on me. I told them to go back and get their mother while I cleaned myself as best I could. My daughter came to the restroom and suggested she follow me closely out to the car." My friend lamented, "I don't ever want to go out in public again. I am sooo ashamed."

"Wait!" I said. "Think of how the devil wants you to respond to this. He wants you to be consumed with shame and humiliation. He'd like for you to just stay at home and lick your wounds. Do the opposite of what he's trying to accomplish. Don't let him win!"

"I don't know whether I can do that or not, but you're probably right. I'm going to have really pray about this, so I don't totally stay out of public."

The next day Sherry called. "I went to the store and bought some protective underwear. Next time I go out, I'll be prepared."

"Good for you! I'm convinced God is glorified when we refuse to fall apart after terribly embarrassing situations."

The apostle Paul was not referring to this problem, but the Scripture is appropriate: "I have learned to be content whatever the circumstances" (Phil. 4:11). We're challenged to remain undaunted. When we're upset, we're not to whine and complain—even when we encounter humbling experiences.

More Problems!

Still dealing with distasteful episodes, I'll throw caution to the wind and bring up another unpleasant aspect of aging. Older citizens often have a problem with gas. It does nothing to help solve the energy crisis as well as contributes to air pollution! We clear our throats or shuffle our feet in an attempt to pretend the noise is coming from somewhere else. We're faced with dealing with bottom burping, or noises resembling an old-fashioned coffee percolator. About the only thing we can do is to dismiss it with a nervous laugh. Though embarrassment is likely to linger, we can refuse to let it control us.

I sense the enemy sitting nearby with a smirk on his face, whispering, "Now aren't you dignified, Big Shot? You can't even control your own body." He uses every opportunity to destroy our sense of self-worth. We must refute his mocking by asserting our God-worth.

> "May our Lord Jesus Christ himself and God our Father,
> who has loved us and given us everlasting comfort and
> hope, which we don't deserve, comfort your hearts with
> all comfort, and help you in every good thing you say
> and do" (2 Thess. 2:16–17 TLB).

One way to defeat Satan in his dastardly plan is to keep from reacting in anger and/or humiliation. Shame, frustration, and self-pity are no better. We recognize this as a part of the process of an older body no longer functioning as it once did. Like the sputtering of an old, dilapidated car, we need more than just a tune-up.

Though this body is wearing out, our attitude doesn't have to wear down. We learn to face adversity with humility, rather than humiliation. We choose to glorify God instead of grumble. By God's grace, we will emerge spiritually and emotionally unscathed.

Taking a Different Look

God can even use this problem of aging as a part of His plan to work on our attitudes. It is a time when we have to deal with pride. Our egos are stomped in the dirt with flatulence and cracked pitchers. Even a world-class celebrity would have difficulty feeling so all-fired important if he has to deal with this problem in public. This may be a time to smile and say, "Oh well," and graciously accept this as an aspect of this transition.

Having taken a look at a leaky or worthless pitcher, we find a counterpart to this dilemma. We can be filled with the Living Water Jesus spoke about when talking to the woman at the well. This water can be poured it out, but it never leaks out. How beautiful—to be a vessel to hold refreshing water that overflows into the lives of others.

Hold On to Joy

My husband, Carey, had a great sense of humor. He could laugh at himself in spite of monumental problems. When he was diagnosed with cancer and had to have a portion of his colon removed, he shrugged. "It's really no big deal. It's only a punctuation change. I used to have a colon and now I have a semi-colon."

In time, the disease so ravaged his body, he had to have a colostomy. Harry Brand, Carey's friend and surgeon, told him that if he went into remission, he could reverse the colostomy. The problem was a hassle to deal with, but Carey handled it well. A few months after the surgery, he phoned Dr. Brand. "Is this Harry's Body Shop? I have a hole in my muffler and need a new tail pipe. How soon can I get it fixed?"

"You crazy Looney guy, you'll just have to hang in there."

Sadly, Carey never went into remission to allow the surgery, though he held tenaciously to his ability to cause others to chuckle or smile. When he went in for chemo treatments, he often took roses or miniature candy bars to share with the staff and patients.

One day he changed into his clown costume before going in the treatment room. It was another effort to lighten the moods of those lined up in chairs to receive their chemo.

One of the nurses told him, "It always makes me feel good when I see your name on my chart for the day." Carey told jokes and lifted the spirits of those around him, until others began to add their little bits of humor to brighten their day in that dismal place.

We're to Stay Filled with Living Water

We need to look for opportunities to bring joy into the lives of others. Bubbling springs of joy flowing from deep within refreshes others. This is to be poured out, rather than leak out. It's good to water someone's flowers or their good points by saying things that are uplifting. We should resist watering the weeds—the things that are downgrading—the things they've done or said that we don't like.

Rivers of Living Water may well represent the joy of the Holy Spirit flowing out of our innermost being. We can make it a game, a concerted effort to look for things to laugh about. The enemy tries to steal our joy because laughter is good medicine. "Always be full of joy in the Lord. I say it again—rejoice!" (Phil. 4:4 NLT).

Small Things Count

We can spread happiness—even if it's just a cup of cold water given in the name of Jesus. It is so rewarding to surprise others with thoughtful little gifts and acts of kindness. Clean and funny stories make others laugh. (Nothing seems much more entertaining than to relate silly things about yourself.) Once Carey said, "Louise, you don't have to tell every dumb mistake you ever made."

"Perhaps not," I explained. "but when I do, I think others identify with me and are relieved that they're not the only ones to pull crazy stunts."

Anointed with Joy

We are not pleasant to be around when we're filled with discouragement and can't hold Living Water. There are those who yearn for anything that will quench their spiritual thirst. God's blessings are far more refreshing than mountain spring water.

Years ago we sang a neat little song. "I'm a little teapot short and stout, tip me over and pour me out."

When we are filled with love and joy, we can pour it into the lives of those around us. Bubbling joy causes people to want to drink this refreshing water. It fills rather than drains.

Be Filled with Living Water

My niece, Claire, taught in a Christian school. She had six Chinese students who had been adopted by American families. When she and I talked about somewhere we could go on a mission strip, she said she would like to go to China. She particularly wanted to visit the orphanage where her students had lived in order to get in touch with their roots. So the decision was made.

While we were in China, we visited a tea room where we were served different kinds of tea. Our hostess explained the rituals associated with each flavor. She served a jasmine tea in a simple clay pot, explaining they always used the same pot to serve that tea, as it absorbed more flavor each time it was brewed. The following night, Claire had a dream in which God told her she was like that little clay pot, absorbing more and more of the love of Jesus.

The next day, she wanted to go shopping to look for one of those little clay teapots as a reminder of her dream. She found one at the market and brought it back to the States as a souvenir.

Shortly after we returned, Claire was diagnosed with cancer and died within a year. They asked me to speak at her funeral.

I took the little teapot from her home and explained how God had shown Claire she was like that little teapot, saturated with the love of God. As we left the funeral that day, it slipped from the bag and shattered on the ground. I was startled, but later, the significance hit.

The teapot represented Claire's body, which had also been shattered—releasing her spirit to go back to God who gave it. The brokenness exposed the flavor inside. The fragrance of God's love that flowed from Claire's heart will continue to live on, far beyond her short time here on this earth.

I miss Claire very much. Sometimes I get misty-eyed thinking of this loss, but I still take sips of the joy and love she brought into my life. The Living Water from her life is still watering my soul and God is taking care of my tears.

> "For the Lamb at the center of the throne will be their
> shepherd; 'he will lead them to springs of living water.'
> 'And God will wipe away every tear from their eyes'"
> (Rev. 7:17).

Let Living Water Overflow

Keep the welcome mat out, Lord. I don't anticipate a long wait. Fill
me Holy Spirit—fill this thirsting of my soul. As I am filled, let my
cup of joy run over and springs of Living Water splash over those
surrounding me.

LIFE APPLICATION

1. How did you respond to embarrassing situations that you've experienced in your life?
2. Can embarrassment be used to humble you rather than humiliate you?
3. How can you defeat Satan's attempts to upset you about the challenges of growing older?
4. How can you keep from wearing down when your body is wearing out?
5. How can you glorify God by remaining steadfast in these trying times?
6. What does Living Water mean to you?
7. Can you think of new ways to spread joy in the lives of others?
8. What do you think it means to come to Jesus to drink?
9. Are you becoming more and more saturated with the love of Jesus?
10. Do you know someone who has poured their life into others?

24

PROBLEMS WITH THE OLD TICKER

... the wheel broken at the well ...
Ecclesiastes 12:6

This wheel Solomon spoke of could be symbolic of the heart pumping life-giving blood throughout the body. The heart, our most vital organ, is our source of life. If the heartbeat is stilled, life-sustaining blood grows stagnant and death is imminent as every cell in the body fades into death from lack of nutrients and oxygen.

The heart is nestled at the very core of our being. Astonishingly, a heartbeat is detected earlier than nine weeks of pregnancy. It begins to beat within the fetus even before the brain develops.

At the amazing moment when the doctor's stethoscope picks up the rhythm of a heartbeat inside the womb, life can be celebrated.

The fetus grows beneath the mother's heart and with that close proximity it initiates the bonding process between mother and child. My daughter-in-law placed a recording of a heartbeat in the crib of her newborn as a source of comfort—trusting the transition from beneath her heart to the outside world would not be so abrupt. The steady and ongoing heartbeat whispers, "I'm here, I'm here, I'm here."

The Heart and Our Emotions

The Bible identifies our heart as the cradle of our emotions, the wellspring of our feelings of joy and sorrow, excitement and fear, bitterness and peace, hate and love. The heart responds and transmits emotions to the rest of our body. We are instructed to guard this emotional center with upmost care. "A man's heart determines his speech" (Matt. 12:34 TLB). Whatever is bottled up in our heart will eventually spew out of our mouths. We must refuse to allow our hearts to be hardened by the world and instead choose to be changed within to become like the tender heart of Jesus.

Bad emotions, emitting from our heart, affect our relationship with God as well as others. Scripture speaks of those who outwardly appear to be honoring God but their hearts are nowhere in sight. If we line up our body, soul, and spirit with the Father, Son, and Holy Spirit, we will be pure in heart. The continuity of our lives will be synchronized with the heartbeat of God.

Disgruntled people with bad attitudes expose their hearts sooner or later by the things they say. Evil thoughts conceived in the heart slither out, sometimes between clenched teeth. The old saying, "Sticks and stones may break my bones, but words can never hurt me," is grossly misleading. Wounds of the flesh heal much quicker and easier than heart wounds. God evaluates our words carefully. "It's your heart, not the dictionary, that gives meaning to your words" (Matt. 12:34 MSG). The wonder is that God can take a stony heart and exchange it for one that is tender.

Physical Manifestations

Our heart responds in different ways as we think of something fearful, peaceful, or joyful. If you could imagine someone giving you a large sum of money, your heart is apt to leap in excitement. If you think of someone trying to break into your home on a dark night, no doubt your heart will pound with fear. Experiment by imagining different situations. Pay attention to the reaction of the heart. It responds in an emotional way, and our bodies follow suit in conjunction with the signals the heart sends out. When we have fear in our hearts, our bodies may tremble and we get cold chills. The hair on the nape of our necks may actually stand on end.

When we feel great compassion or love, we talk about our hearts melting or being tender. This can motivate us to hold someone who is hurting in our arms to comfort them. When others are going through difficult times we want to reach out and touch them.

Sometimes hearts become hard when people are offended. Muscles tense, jaws and fists clench. Hardened hearts refuse to be touched by someone else's pain.

When we grieve, we think of a broken or a heavy heart. As tears flow, our bodies often feel weak. On the other hand, when we are upbeat, we talk about being lighthearted and we become energized.

Don't Lose Heart

When our children were ages three, two, and another in the "oven," we made the exciting decision to go to Japan as missionaries. In preparation, we decided to have a garage sale to dispose of most of our belongings to raise money to go. We set up long tables in the basement of our home and loaded them with household goods. People from church were given first choice to purchase what they wanted including furniture in the rooms upstairs. Carey put a jar on one of the long tables and asked people to pick whatever they wanted and put what they felt the item was worth in the jar. I was a bit skeptical, but He assured me people would be generous because it was for a worthy cause.

After the sale, we stared at each other in disbelief as we counted the money. There was only pocket change. We struggled to keep from being downhearted and resentful.

We loaded our children and the essentials we'd decided to keep in the car and headed for Texas. We arrived at a church that agreed to help us financially until we raised sufficient funds for our support.

After six weeks, they'd given us no money and we were utterly broke. We slept on the floor of the church building with our children. We felt abandoned and uncared for. We came to the conclusion that if the church was that unconcerned while we were in their midst, we might well be left stranded in Japan with no money to make it back to the States. We decided not to go overseas as missionaries. It was heartrending as we experienced the death of a vision.

For a while, we surmised the enemy had blocked our way. Later, however, we saw God's fingerprints. Carey decided to go back to school and finish his doctorate in counseling. He would spend the rest of his life ministering to others. God used the entire situation to get us to the place He planned for us.

A Light Heart—or Enthusiasm

Before Carey became my husband, he sat in front of me at a college football game. Since I'd been a cheerleader, I was naturally animated. Carey asked me for a date a few weeks later and chuckled about how loud I cheered our team. "I started to turn around at the game and say, 'Lady, if you lose your voice, you'll probably find it in my ear.'"

It is my nature to get excited and be enthusiastic. Being high-spirited is fun and seems to be a part of my DNA. Enthusiasm lifts me on the wings of expectation and I become lighthearted.

Don't Lose Hope

It is somewhat common for older people to appear heavyhearted and lose their zest for living. Hope drains from their faces, leaving them with furrowed brows and downturned mouths. Their expressions sag as well as body parts. I'd much rather resemble my uncle who has crinkles encircling his sparkling eyes that deepened from years of laughter.

Some older citizens contend they are justified in becoming discouraged because their bodies don't function properly anymore. As the years march on, debilitating factors are like snipers—shooting down one organ after another. There's a tendency to lose heart. If this begins to happen, let it be a signal for us to look for things that will encourage us. Better still, be a catalyst to encourage others.

Pessimism is the result of a heavy heart and is generally

accompanied with a lack of initiative and energy. A heavy heart is like a bucket of lead, pressing down on our chest.

A Lonely Heart

Soon after a spouse dies, loneliness often moves in as a haunting companion. Some widows or widowers compromise their convictions in an attempt to avoid being alone by immediately getting involved with someone else. It is wise to get the counsel of godly friends. I'm aware of several who felt certain the Lord was leading them to marry very quickly after the death of their spouse. They didn't listen to advice from others. Sadly, some later regretted they'd let their loneliness overrule wisdom and counsel.

Those who are suddenly faced with living alone do yearn for companionship. But activities can serve as a diversion to occupy our minds and keep us from experiencing a lonely heart. When we are feeling alone, it's good to look for something productive we can do. Go out to eat with a friend, invite people in for a meal or a visit. Find others who are alone and plan things to do together. Keep a list of possible activities you can get involved in when your heart begins to feel lonely—things that will lift your spirits.

I find that when I isolate myself, the devil uses this as a time to walk all over me. God is our shield and protector. He not only sent Jesus, but He also sent us the Comforter, the Holy Spirit, to be with us as we grieve our losses. However, we not only need spiritual help, but we need people with skin on to keep us company. It is helpful to find others who have been through similar experiences so we can encourage one another and not have to bear our grief alone.

A Heart of Grief and Loss

Wise doctors may suggest family members give their suffering loved ones permission to die. My friend, June, prayed day after day that her critically ill mother would be healed. It broke her heart to think of losing her mom. One day, while June was sitting by her side in the hospital, her mother rallied for a few moments and turned to her and said, "Please let me go." June was shocked when she realized her mom was ready to die yet she'd been begging God to let her live. She thought for a few moments, took a deep breath, and uttered, "Lord, if it's time for her to go, please take her."

Within hours, her mother's wish was granted and she passed on to a better life. June was able to allow her mother's wishes to overrule her own heart's desire. When we lose a loved one, the empty place in our hearts leaves us brokenhearted.

The Challenge to Adapt and Adjust

My mother asked to go into a nursing home after Dad's death because she was losing her hearing and eyesight. There, she busied herself in helping set tables in the dining room, pulling weeds in the flower beds, working crossword puzzles, and reading. She told us before she moved into the home, "I've already made up my mind, I'll be happy there."

I was visiting her one day and the man in an adjoining room kept hollering. I asked Mom if he did this often. She said, "Yes, he yells quite a bit."

I was somewhat alarmed. "Doesn't that bother you?"

She smiled and said, "No, I'm just glad I don't hear very well."

Mom had been in the home eighteen months when one morning she started having chest pains and walked to the front desk to tell them. The staff had her lie down and called an ambulance to rush her to the hospital. Then, they phoned my sister and brother who lived nearby. My two siblings hurried to the emergency room to be with her. Mom turned to my brother and said, "I surely hope I don't mess up your plans to leave on vacation this weekend." She didn't. She died before noon. Even in the critical hours before death, her heart was concerned about others. My sister-in-law remarked: "Wasn't that just like Mom? Anytime she decided to do anything positive, she never wasted time following through with her plans." Congestive heart failure had stolen her life, but couldn't touch her heart of love that was concerned about others.

The day of her funeral, when we started to walk into the church building, a niece pointed to the sky and exclaimed, "Look, God sent flowers." We all looked toward the heavens and were amazed to see a rainbow circling above the church. That beautiful phenomenon remained until we were ready to leave the cemetery. In an amazing way, God comforted our hearts in a way we couldn't have anticipated.

Our broken hearts aren't like Humpty Dumpty's that "all the king's horses and all the king's men, couldn't put Humpty together again." Our Savior carefully mends broken hearts, using his love as the super glue to hold us together. "He existed before anything else, and he holds all creation together" (Col. 1:17 NLT).

If Everything Goes Kaput

"My flesh and my heart may fail, but God is the strength of my heart and my portion forever" (Ps. 73:26). The heart cannot be recycled. The new heart God gives us is not powered by a signal from the brain or by a pacemaker. It is God's perfect heart transplant that will beat throughout all eternity.

LIFE APPLICATION

1. Do you know of someone whose heart has been deceived?
2. Which emotion do you have the most difficulty controlling?
3. Can a compassionate heart influence our emotions too much?
4. Do you make it a habit to ask to be led by the Spirit of God?
5. What kinds of situations are most likely to trigger bad emotions in you?
6. Describe the difference between a heart of stone—a hard heart and a heart of flesh—and one that is compassionate and loving.
7. Describe the difference between a heavy heart and a light heart.
8. Do you ever do things for others to get your mind off your own broken heart?
9. How can God be the strength of your heart?
10. Can you imagine your heart beating in sync with God's?

25

FROM DUST TO DUST

... the dust returns to the ground it came from ...
Ecclesiastes 12:7

God formed man from the dust of the earth and in the end, man will return full cycle. The Lord created us to be biodegradable. Under my bed I find "dust bunnies" galore. I dare not disturb them. They might be the makings of a man. But then again, who knows whether he's coming or going?

Flesh and blood are expendable, but this does not indicate our lives are "dirt cheap." "For you were bought at a price; therefore glorify God in your body and in your spirit, which are God's" (1 Cor. 6:20 NKJV).

Though this body of weakness will decompose as dust, our spirits are everlasting. They remain totally alive to break free to be lifted on wings of angels to an eternal home. Our bodies return to the earth as ground cover, but our eternal spirit returns to its roots, its place of origin.

Henry Wadsworth Longfellow wrote, "Dust thou art was not spoken of the soul." It is reassuring to know that only the shell of mankind is expendable. Jesus gave His life to make it possible for our spirits to live with Him forever.

What Can God Do with Ordinary Clay?

We usually think of a person who says he has feet of clay as one who is aware of his human weaknesses. My feet of clay extend all the way up to my armpits!

There is a graphic illustration of a potter in the book of Jeremiah—a story illustrating God doing a makeover with a nation.

> "This is the word that came to Jeremiah from the LORD: 'Go down to the potter's house, and there I will give you my message.' So I went down to the potter's house, and I saw him working at the wheel. But the pot he was shaping from the clay was marred in his hands; so the potter formed it into another pot, shaping it as it seemed best to him. Then the word of the LORD came to me. He said, 'Can I not do with you, Israel, as this potter does?'" (Jer. 18:1−6).

If God can squash a nation and remake it, surely He can do the same with you and me. Many times God has had to go with plan "B" in my life because I've resisted His touch to mold me the way He first planned.

God knows and understands the stages of life we go through and He stands ready to remold us at any age, even when we're old and have made poor choices. "For he knows how weak we are; he remembers we are only dust" (Ps. 103:14 NLT).

God has had me on the potter's wheel for well over the biblical lifespan of threescore and ten years. I want to remain pliable in the Master's hand. Let Him shape me as He will.

In the New Testament, St. Paul talks of how God uses fallible human beings to carry out His divine plan. "But we have this treasure [the gospel] in jars of clay to show that this all-surpassing power is from God and not from us" (2 Cor. 4:7). At Hidden Manna, we had a clay jar that had been cracked and repaired. My friend said, "That cracked pot reminds me of my life—broken but restored by God's almighty grace."

Don't Argue with God

Have you wondered why God gave different ones of us the personalities we have? We trust our Heavenly Father knew perfectly well how He wanted to put us together. He gave us the talents we have. How foolish it would be to quarrel with the Creator, as if to challenge whether He knew what He was doing. This would be like questioning Michelangelo's artistic ability to paint the Sistine chapel.

Why not thank God for our features—even those we don't care for, accepting that He knew what He was doing. Instead of grumbling and complaining, we ask the Father for His grace to shine through our imperfections. "And the parts we think are less honorable we treat with special honor" (1 Cor. 12:23).

When my son, Paul, was in the first grade, some children in his class were making fun of a classmate who had crossed eyes. The teacher interrupted their mocking and explained that everyone has some kind of flaws. Paul raised his hand and asked to show the children his unusual toes. The teacher invited him to come up to the front of the room and pull off his shoes, while his classmates gathered around. Paul pointed at his feet and showed the children two toes on each foot that were grown together. The teacher hoped that once the children realized each person is different, they would accept everyone, just as they are.

Now, Paul laughs. "My grandfather had toes that were grown together on one foot; mine are grown together on both feet. While the webbed toes on my feet allow me to swim well, my grandfather's webbed toes on one foot enabled him to swim circles around me."

God Has a Purpose for Each of Us

I'm not as smart or talented as some of my brothers and sisters. While both my sisters were valedictorians of their high school graduating class, I was not. My brother was the "fair-haired" gifted artist and leader in the school and community, but I wasn't. When I finally accepted the unique way God made me, I developed the talents He had given me and looked to God for my self-image.

I'm so thankful God gave us all the same message of hope— through His Word and His Son, Jesus. He's not partial to anyone. There's a special place for each of us in His kingdom. God uses all types of individuals as evidence of His creative touch.

Ken Starr, an attorney who was a former Federal Judge and Solicitor General, told about something he experienced in Washington D.C. Ken said, "There was a young man with Down's syndrome who operated the elevator in my building. Every day he greeted me with a huge smile and 'Good morning, Judge, have a wonderful day!' This man set the tone for my day. It saddens me to know that now more than 93 percent of children with Down's syndrome are aborted."

Seed Needs Good Soil

The Word of God is compared to seed. Sometimes that seed falls along the path and is trampled. There are countless millions who have no regard for God's Word and who tread it underfoot. The average Christian home has four Bibles, but it would be interesting to know how many are read on a regular basis. We act as if our Bibles have little value when we fail to study and follow God's commandments. *Lord, don't let our lives become dusty like dust on the Bibles on our shelves because we don't read and study Your Word more. Pick us up, Lord. Dust us off and use us.*

When I smuggle Bibles into a foreign country, I hope they don't get confiscated and destroyed as I go through Customs. The people waiting for these Bibles are fine, fertile soil. One of my friends in China has a Bible her mother hand-copied in its entirety so she could have God's Word for her very own.

Some seeds on the ground don't get adequate rain. They may sprout but quickly wither away. "The seed is the word of God" (Luke 8:11). We need the water of the Holy Spirit for our roots to grow down so we can become strong.

People who are self-reliant are like hard ground refusing to receive the Word.

Even Old Seeds Can Sprout

When the Egyptian pyramids were reopened, archaeologists found seeds that were thousands of years old. When these were planted in good soil and watered, they sprouted, grew, and produced a crop. The Word of God that has lain dormant for years can still take root and grow.

A couple of years ago an older woman from church approached me and asked me to pray that her husband would accept Jesus as Lord. We prayed, and over a year later she asked if I remembered our prayer. I did. She said, "My husband became a Christian a few months later. A short time afterwards, he died—but he died with a strong faith. I had prayed for him for seventy-five years." She had cultivated the soil in her husband and the good seed finally took root. Her prayers had not been in vain. Just as in the natural world, some seed may take root and ripen at a later season. The latter rain of the Spirit prompts them to take root and produce fruit. We've been entrusted with God's Word to plant, knowing only God can make it grow.

Are You Planting Seed?

Personally, I feel my primary gift is one who waters and encourages others. I like to take struggling Christians under my wing. As a mentor, I feel the need to teach younger Christians how to pull out weeds of anger, shame, and unforgiveness.

Lessons Learned at the Retreat

Jill came to Hidden Manna, our retreat center, wanting to regain the relationship she'd once had with God. She'd read the story of Jeremiah watching the potter remake the clay pot and she was ready for God to remake her.

As she stood on the porch of the Casa, our Golden Retriever, Sassy, came to the gate and barked. A moment later, Sassy trotted up to her side briefly and then went back to the gate, turned around, and barked again.

Jill thought, *This is strange, but I think the dog wants me to follow her.* She walked over and patted Sassy and then followed her deep into the woods. Sassy led her to a wooden cross where people went to pray and meditate. The area had become neglected and overgrown. When Sassy lay down by the cross, a chill went down Jill's back. She felt God whisper, "That's your life—full of weeds."

She lay down at the foot of the cross and cried as she identified and pulled the weeds she realized she'd allowed to grow in her life. Her life had been good soil, but she'd failed to nurture godly virtues and careless weeds of neglect had taken over.

When she pulled the last weed, she felt a great weight lifted from her shoulders. The weeds that had strangled God's place of priority in her life were gone. She would no longer allow the worldly weeds to distract her from serving the Lord.

New Birth at Any Age

"For you have been born again, not of perishable seed, but of imperishable, through the living and enduring word of God" (1 Peter 1:23). Young women produce an egg [seed] that is capable of becoming a baby. There comes a time when age stops this cycle. But the Word of God, planted in one's heart, will continue to produce lives that will live throughout eternity.

This old shell of a body will return to dust and lie dormant until God's appointed time. I'd like to think this clay pot has been shaped and used for the purpose God intended—either filled to the brim with the seed of the Word, or filled with Living Water to nurture tender plants that will continue to grow and bear fruit long after we've passed this way.

Life Application

1. Explain some ways our spirit is different from our earthly body.
2. Are there areas in your life where God may be trying to reshape you?
3. Do you ever feel you are too old to change?
4. Have you ever wondered why God made you as He did?
5. Can you think of how God can use something you don't like about yourself to accomplish something good?
6. Have you ever seen God use an unlikely person for a great purpose?
7. Was there a time when you felt cheated because of the things that happened in your life?
8. Why should we never stop praying for someone to be saved?
9. Can you think of someone you need to pray for to become a Christian?
10. Are there weeds in your life that you need to pull out?

26

THE SPIRIT SLIPS AWAY QUIETLY

The spirit returns to God who gave it.
Ecclesiastes 12:7

Soon the wheel will be broken at the well, the silver cord will be severed, and the spirit will vacate this old body. Similar to a hermit crab, our spirit occupies this shell for a while, but God doesn't intend for us to live in this limited space indefinitely. We were created to live in a much larger and better environment. Our spirit will be set free to be transported faster than the speed of light to live forever in the presence of the Great I AM. This body will have served its purpose and will be ready to be discarded. But this is not true of the spirit. It will spiral into heaven, leaving this shell behind. This will be the time of the great exodus.

Different Kinds of Spirits

We cautiously examine the Scriptures, making sure we are filled with the right kind of spirit. There are good and bad spirits. There are deceptive and lying spirits, vile and evil spirits, and those that are unclean. But, as children of God, we have access to His Holy Spirit that can fill and empower us, guide us, and comfort us.

We are given the Holy Spirit at baptism, but Luke tells us we can also ask for it.

> "Even though you are bad, you know how to give good
> things to your children. How much more your heavenly
> Father will give the Holy Spirit to those who ask him!"
> (Luke 11:13 NCV).

As we respond in obedience to the Father, we find His Spirit living in us as evidence that we are citizens of His heavenly kingdom. D. L. Moody, a famous evangelist, was asked why he continually prayed to be filled with the Holy Spirit. He replied, "Because I leak!"

We ask God to help us live in such a way that we do not grieve or quench the Spirit. We long for every possible gift and resource, to live in such a way that glorifies our Heavenly Father.

Nothing is more important than our preparation to live forever. God lavishly provides us with His Holy Spirit, to lead us into all Truth. His gift equips us to live far better than we could ever do on our own. "Those who have lived the right way will walk out into resurrection Life" (John 5:29 MSG).

Forever Friends

There are times I've met believers I'd love to know better but they live a distance away. After a brief meeting I can say, "I haven't gotten to know you as well as I'd like. But over there on the other side, there's surely a grassy slope, just beyond the river. After the sound of the trumpet, meet me there. We'll get better acquainted and we can visit as long and as much as we want."

The Books Will Be Opened

A time of judgment is coming when the books will be opened. One book records the things we've done in this life and will determine rewards we will receive. We'll stand trembling before Almighty God as He reviews our words and deeds. We can thank God, however, that there will be page after page that is blank because we've confessed the sins that were once written there. Because of the sacrifice of Jesus, they have been blotted out—never to be held against us.

On that day, the Book of Life will be opened, which contains a list of God's adopted children. Those names are written in indelible ink by the finger of God. Nothing can erase them. By believing and trusting in Jesus we've made sure our names have been recorded so we can stand in the winner's circle.

No Target for Satan

Remarkably, when the spirit slips through these cracked and broken vessels, it flies away as silently as butterfly wings with none of the trappings of this earth.

> "For instance, we know that when these bodies of ours are taken down like tents and folded away, they will be replaced by resurrection bodies in heaven—God-made, not handmade—and we'll never have to relocate our tents again" (2 Cor. 5:1–2 MSG).

Satan cannot afflict a dead body with pain, disease, or weakness. When a believer dies, friends and family may consider it a defeat—that the person has fallen prey to the devil's schemes. Initially, it may look as if Satan has won the prize package. But the enemy will discover the contents are gone. He's left holding an empty container of dirt filtering through his wicked fingers. That which has been born of the Spirit, cannot be touched or harmed by any demon of hell.

There is a Time to Release the Spirit

As Carey's health declined, we'd done everything we knew to stop the spread of the disease of cancer, but we determined to trust God to hold his lifeline in His hands. We were forced to bow in humble submission as we watched Carey graduate *summa cum laude* and accept the invitation to "come on home."

> "So friends, confirm God's invitation to you, his choice of you. Don't put it off; do it now. Do this, and you'll

have your life on a firm footing, the streets paved and the way wide open into the eternal kingdom of our Master and Savior, Jesus Christ" (2 Peter 1:10–11 MSG).

When that time comes, we'll concede nothing we endured has been too great a price to pay. No pain has been too unbearable, no struggle too difficult, no trial too long, no sorrow too deep. All struggles combined are nothing compared to the glorious reward that awaits God's children.

The shroud of death and all it implies will drop away to be replaced by a robe of righteousness. There will be no need to bemoan what we have been, for we will discover what we've inherited. We will loosen our clenched fists that have held on to this life in order to grasp something far better.

Shame and regret will be banished from our memories as our robes have been washed in the blood of the Lamb.

> "You should clothe yourselves instead with beauty that comes from within, the unfading beauty of a gentle and quiet spirit, which is so precious To God: (1. Peter 3:4).

Pain will evaporate in the light of the Son. We will rise up in blessed relief, knowing the serpent has been cast down. He will never again be able to rob, kill, and destroy anything good in our lives. He's led us astray for the last time. We'll no longer be deceived by his schemes.

Time and age will never cause us to stoop. The weight of all our concerns and the cares of this world will be lifted and left behind. We'll be rid of all burdens. We'll stand tall and straight, and our strength will equal our days. Rather than be cowed by fear, our whole being will ripple with bold confidence. This earth and its troubles will never again shake us.

We will witness and hear the reverberating voices of those bowing before the throne throughout eternity praising God, "Holy, holy, holy is the Lord God Almighty. He was, he is and he is coming" (Rev 4:8 NCV).

The Old Cocoon Drops Away

On that day, our spirit will be set free and the old cocoon, gray with death and crackled by age, can no longer restrain the spirit from returning to God who gave it. The wind of the Holy Spirit will scatter the dust that remains and all the dirty limitations that have been imposed on this mortal body.

Faith will erupt into reality. Hope will burst forth into full possession of more than we ever dreamed. The updraft from the wind of the Spirit will continue to lift us higher.

Every burden will have been lifted from our shoulders. No heart will ever be stilled or broken. Can you imagine any greater freedom than being free from fear, free from financial concerns, living in the land where God owns the cattle on a thousand hills? There will never be any limits or shortages of anything good. Even our thought-life will be pure. There'll be no jealousy of those who are permitted to sit close to the throne. We'll simply rejoice in the mercy and grace our Father has shown to us as we understand the depth of His love for each individual. A new power is in operation. "The Spirit of life in Christ, like a strong wind, has magnificently cleared the air, freeing you from a fated lifetime of brutal tyranny at the hands of sin and death" (Rom. 8:2 MSG).

> "So don't you see that we don't owe this old do-it-yourself life one red cent? There's nothing in it for us, nothing at all. The best thing to do is give it a decent burial and get on with your new life. God's Spirit beckons. There are things to do and places to go!" (Rom. 8:12–14 MSG)

Chills of anticipation likely sweep over us as we look forward to the time when our spirits will be set free—free indeed.

LIFE APPLICATION

1. Would we be so concerned about this body if we realized the real significance of the spirit within?
2. What are you doing to produce more of the fruit of the Spirit in your life?
3. Explain how you have seen bad spirits at work in someone's life.
4. Have you thought about how wonderful it will be when Satan can longer harass us after our spirit leaves the body?
5. What does it mean to have a free spirit?
6. Do you believe that eternal life is worth far more than the price we had to pay for it?
7. What do you look forward to understanding in heaven?
8. What will it be like to have no cares in heaven?
9. What specific pain or trouble will you be most grateful for not having to deal with?
10. What does it mean to realize that every time you confess a sin, God totally erases it from His record book and never remembers it again?

27

MEANINGLESS BECOME MEANINGFUL

"Meaningless! Meaningless!" says the Teacher. "Everything is meaningless!"
Ecclesiastes 12:8

When Adam and Eve sinned in the Garden of Eden, they were sentenced to live in the clutches of aging and death. This silent destroyer began to claim his victims, from one generation to the next, until now he's staring at some of us as we enter these later years. Satan takes advantage of this curse of aging and sneers as we struggle with bodies that are wearing out and breaking down. If we only look at life from a physical viewpoint, it *is* meaningless.

This may well be the most challenging time of our lives, but God never intended for it to be meaningless. Regardless of what happens to this old earth-suit, we can be confident our compassionate God is not playing a cruelty joke on his older children by creating sagging body parts with wrinkles and malfunctioning organs. God may allow this to be a humbling experience, but He never intended for it to be humiliating.

Metamorphosis

God takes what Satan intended to be a devastating blow and uses it for a metamorphic process—a time to develop something beautiful on the

217

inside, while the outer man's purpose is winding down. Envision the spirit as a proverbial butterfly, developing inside and growing more beautiful every day.

A light bulb switches on above my head as Scripture comes alive.

> "So we're not giving up. How could we! Even though on the outside it often looks like things are falling apart on us, on the inside, where God is making new life, not a day goes by without his unfolding grace" (2 Cor. 4:16 MSG).

Concentrate on what really matters in this transmutation. It's time for us to pray for God to polish us until His love shines clearly through us.

During the transformation inside a cocoon, the caterpillar sends out antibodies in an attempt to destroy the butterfly. It hampers its growth somewhat, but ultimately the new creature grows stronger until the caterpillar melts into a soupy nutrient the butterfly feeds on. The focus of our lives is to nourish this beautiful spirit within as the wings of victory are unfolding.

Beauty on the Inside

My niece, Celia, came to me one day and said, "Open your mouth."

I opened it a bit.

"Open it wide." Though I didn't understand, I did what she asked.

"Ah, you're beautiful in there too."

Thanks, I needed that.

Life would be meaningless if, when we leave this planet, blank eyes were left staring at only bits of significance we've left behind. Thankfully, we still have time to touch others and possibly influence them to choose Jesus as Lord and open the door to eternal life. The bits and pieces of things we say and do are a strong influence on others.

What would people miss if you were suddenly whisked out of the picture? If our main concern has been on our physical body and material things, we'll end up as mortals whose worth has depreciated with time. But if we dedicate our lives to being servants of God, we'll find ourselves reaping eternal benefits. We can stay cool in spite of hot flashes that are a distraction to us.

Remember the inspiring movie, *It's a Wonderful Life*? Jimmy Stewart was allowed to look back in a vision and see how different things would have been if he'd never lived. Would there be an empty void if we never touched people's lives? Is the world a better place because we were here? "They share freely and give generously to those in need. Their good deeds will be remembered forever. They will have influence and honor" (Ps. 112:9 NLT).

There are many contributions we can make at this stage of the life that will have a great impact on others. I'm not talking about humongous accomplishments or stashes of wealth, but rather sprinkles of joy and showers of blessings overflowing from our hearts to God and others. It's wise to impact the culture rather than allowing culture to determine who we have become. God has designed this powerful force to come from the inside and flow out into the world.

In order to prepare for a meaningful future, it is important to create a meaningful today. Begin to make mental notes of ways to bless others. Consider how much it would mean if we took a few minutes every day to express gratitude to God and others—for the way people have enriched our lives. Send a note, an email, or give someone a phone call. "Yes, you will be enriched in every way so that you can always be generous. And when we take your gifts to those who need them, they will thank God" (2 Cor. 9:11 NLT).

Surprising Gifts

Surprises are especially meaningful. Sarah had an old, beat-up chair in her attic. It had been a gift to her aunt from students and teachers when she served as a school principal during World War II. Sarah's daughter, Charla, had chosen it as the one thing she wanted when her aunt passed away. The chair fell out of a truck when they were moving and broke into several pieces. Not wanting to dispose of it, they put it in the attic and subsequently forgot it for decades.

Charla became a school principal. While she was on vacation, her mother took the broken chair, had it restored, and placed it in her office at school for her to discover when she returned from her trip. Charla wept in gratitude over her mother's thoughtfulness in restoring this sentimental treasure.

Send Messages of Encouragement

My husband kept a special file folder with encouraging notes others had written him. He got them out on days he felt discouraged. I found these after his death, along with silly notes and poems I'd written to him over the years.

Far too often, I've been guilty of thinking of things I *should* do and say and somehow kept putting them off, never getting around to following through. One day, my son, Paul, said, "Mom, somehow I get the feeling you think you get brownie points just for thinking about doing nice things." Ouch! Guilty as charged.

It is time to give our attention to what God would have us do, right now. Yesterdays may be filled with lost opportunities, but today gives us a chance to live with no regrets.

Are There Things to Let Go?

Al came to the retreat center and sat with us outside on the deck for the morning devotional. He shared how others had taken advantage of him and misfortunes had plagued him in his business. He was convinced the world had not been fair to him. We acknowledged that the world *is* often unfair.

> "The world is unprincipled. It's dog eat dog out there! The world doesn't fight fair. But we don't live or fight our battles that way—never have, never will" (2 Cor. 10:3 MSG).

In a sense, much of Al's life seemed meaningless.

As he shared his struggles, I was distracted by a dead leaf

dangling from a spider web above his head. When I could no longer sit still, I got up, went over, and yanked it down and apologized for my strange behavior that interrupted the devotional.

After our final prayer, Al went back to the Casa, one of our retreat houses, to sit outside on the glider. A gust of wind blew a shower of leaves in front of him. He noticed how lifeless the leaves were—all crackly and brown. He saw a correlation with his life. Many "dead leaves" from his past needed to be blown away. He symbolically lifted each issue up and asked for the wind of the Holy Spirit to blow them from his life.

A tree shedding its leaves reminded him that old leaves had to drop in order to offer a place for new ones to grow. Al understood. It was time to start building new experiences. "Your old life is dead. Your new life, which is your real life—even though invisible to spectators—is with Christ in God" (Col. 3:3 MSG).

Redeem the Time

We can redeem the time by concentrating on a meaningful life today. We're to discard dead issues. We're not just biding our time. Our lives here are not a dress rehearsal, but we're on stage before a live audience. It's imperative to make these remaining days meaningful for those who watch and follow us. There's no need to lament over times we've messed up in the past. This is a new day and we can still utilize the marvelous gift of life God has given us.

Rather than our efforts being meaningless, we determine to work with God in order for our lives to be fulfilling and worthwhile. "Blessed rest from their hard, hard work. None of what they've done is wasted; God blesses them for it all in the end" (Rev. 14:13 MSG).

Make Life Meaningful for Others

Our friend, Eddie, spent his life reaching out to underprivileged children who lived on the streets of New York City. He traveled across the nation to raise funds so these children could have an opportunity to get out of the city and go to a summer camp—a fun place where they could enjoy God's great outdoors, but they would also learn about Jesus.

When Eddie drove down the streets on the East Side, he honked the horn of his old bus. Children ran after him as if he were the Pied Piper. He handed out brochures, advertising two weeks of free camping which would get them away from the slums into the glorious countryside.

He visited us in Denver on one of his cross-country treks and commented, "It will be so good when God calls me home. I'm worn out and ready for a long rest." When we went out to see him off the next morning, Carey gasped as he looked at his tires. "Eddie, those tires are worn down to the tread. They will never get you home."

Eddie sighed. "The Lord sent me on this mission, and He knows I don't have money to replace the tires. I'm counting on Him to be with me until I finish my trip."

He wrote us afterward. "The day after arriving home in New Jersey, I went out to my car and found two tires were flat." Eddie worked hard for quite a number of additional years and then, one day, God granted his wish and took him home to rest.

I look forward to meeting him in heaven. He'll probably be followed by a whole passel of children who will be doing cartwheels along the banks of the River of Life. I can almost hear his hearty laughter in the distance as he urges them, "keep on running." Until the end, Eddie's life remained meaningful as he touched countless hundreds of children's lives and changed the destiny of many.

Stay Faithful to the End

We're blessed in knowing we can live each day secure in the fact that if it were our last, it would be fine. I still have projects I'd like to finish, but I hope that's true when the last trumpet sounds. Slowly, resolutely, we march to the sound of a distant drummer, knowing we draw closer to our destination every day. We'll not give up the hope of completing our purpose here victoriously.

It will be wonderful to hear Jesus say, "Come, you who are blessed by my Father; take your inheritance, the kingdom prepared for you since the creation of the world" (Matt. 25:34). This will be what Paul Harvey often referred to as "the rest of the story." This time will be far from meaningless. This "meaningless" world will no longer be listed as our permanent residence. We've prepared to move into a meaningful country of incomparable joy and beauty.

I can't say this road I've traveled has been easy, but I can assure you that following Jesus is gloriously fulfilling. As we fit into God's plans, our mouths will be so filled with laughter our tongues will taste its sweetness. Our hearts can continue to be vessels of peace, pumping love and hope on those surrounding us. No one can convince me this journey has been meaningless!

When we reach the other side, life will never have been so real, light never will have been so bright, or joy so pure. "Now we see only a poor reflection as in a mirror; then we shall see face to face. Now I know in part; then I shall know fully, even as I am fully known" (1 Cor. 13:12). The transformation will be complete. Meaninglessness will have been transformed into meaningfulness.

Life Application

1. Has the enemy chosen to use aging and disabilities to discourage or defeat you?
2. How can you compare the spirit inside to that of a butterfly developing inside a cocoon?
3. Can you think of how God is working inside you to develop a beautiful spirit?
4. Can you see God's purpose in the outer shell (our body) having to drop away in order to release the spirit within?
5. Are there small gifts you can offer to those around you?
6. Can you think of a surprise gift you might offer someone?
7. Is it difficult for you to reach out to others?
8. What could you do today to make life more meaningful for someone?
9. Do you tend to only be concerned about your own problems?
10. What would help you switch meaningless things in your life to make them more meaningful?

28

FINDING THE TREASURE

Solomon concludes his discourse on aging with a profound statement:
Now all has been heard;
here is the conclusion of the matter:
Fear God and keep his commandments,
for this is the whole duty of man
Ecclesiastes 12:13

W hen Solomon targeted the highest goal for our lives, he cautioned us not to depend on our own wits but rather look to Almighty God for guidance. Even the wisest of men don't have enough knowledge to teach us how to live an abundant life.

God's commandments hang from a golden thread of love running throughout the Bible. The substance of God's mandate is to love others as much as we love ourselves. Love includes reverence and honor of God and respect for all His children.

There'll be no need to shop for appropriate clothing to stand before Almighty God. He purchased a robe of righteousness with the price of His Son, Jesus. The blood of Christ saturates the warp and woof of this priceless garment. Like Joseph's coat of many colors, its multiple features represent an incredible gift from a loving Father.

Not only does God furnish us with a robe of righteousness, but He gives us the boldness and wisdom to rule over principalities and powers and the dark evils of this world. This authority also helps us reign over our own bad attitudes and self-serving interests.

Now Is a Time to Hope

We realize that aging is not a time to cope, but a time to hope. "Relax, everything is going to be all right; everything is coming together; open your hearts, love is on its way!" (Jude v. 2 MSG). God's grace is expressed in His unconditional love. He gives rhyme and reason to everything that happens in the challenges of aging.

So, it's time to spend less time in our rocking chairs. We've been rocking back and forth long enough—keeping us busy, but not getting us anywhere. We'll walk away from endless computer games. It will be no problem to shut off the television for a spell in order to make our greatest impact on the world. As we delve into the truths of God's wisdom, we find meaning in this transformation. We're to go with gusto, no turning back. This is not a time to procrastinate. God's grace offers us a window of time for us to respond to His call. It's our opportunity to seize the day!

We find purpose in the aging process, a time of refinement as we release the grip on this world and submit to following the commandments of God. We embrace the maladies of aging and the wasting away of this outer shell, as we understand the resplendent beauty of an immortal spirit that has been developing within. Like the wise virgins, waiting for the bridegroom, we fill our lamps with the oil of the Spirit. We'll keep them burning bright and held high until the door is opened. We pray others will see the light and join the wedding party.

Never Give Up

Though we may be growing older and be a bit weary, we'll never give up. We stand firm with the declaration,

> "So we're not giving up. How could we! Even though on the outside it often looks like things are falling apart on us, on the inside, where God is creating a new life, not a

day goes by without his unfolding grace. ... The things we can't see now will last forever" (2 Cor. 4:16, 18 MSG).

The Holy Spirit has been acting as dialysis to extract the impurities from our souls and constantly cleanse us from the inside out. God sent a fisher of men to reel us in, but then He sent the Holy Spirit to clean us up. I've asked Him to show me every secret sin in my life. *Lord, let me deal with sin now, rather than later! May I empty myself so you can fill me with your Spirit, leaving no room for regret.*

Focus on Things of Real Value

Stories are told of rich families in Europe, fleeing from the enemy during World War II. They loaded silver, jewelry, and expensive items in bags and lugged them along the road. As the days grew long and they became exhausted and worn out, they began to toss these expensive items into the ditches, retaining only food and clothing necessary to survive. We, too, find we've carried baggage that has no lasting value. It has slowed us down and hampered our progress.

We now know God has had purpose in our aging. Our challenge is to ask the Father to reveal what He wants to teach us each step of the way. Though the whole reason our struggles won't be revealed until we stand before the Great White Throne, we pray we've brought glory to Him by completing the work He laid out for us to do.

Nothing matters more at this stage of the game than finding how God wants to put the finishing touches on the spirit residing within in preparation for the new kingdom He prepared for us. The time on the potter's wheel is almost over. We're ready to be placed in the kiln for the last time. These last fiery trials can reveal brilliant colors our Creator painted with His artistic touch.

When the time comes for us to shed these earthly tents, we'll realize we've been away from our real home. Perhaps there won't be yellow ribbons flying from the Tree of Life, but we anticipate a marvelous welcome from those who've gone ahead—those who are waiting and watching. Our citizenship in heaven has been confirmed and we await our rite of passage.

Jesus will be our escort to take us home. He will transform these weak and worn-out bodies and change them into glorious immortal bodies like His own. The power that raised Jesus from the dead will also raise us up. In contrast to Dorothy, in the Wizard of Oz, we'll not walk on a yellow brick road but on streets of pure gold. However, we *will* declare with her, "There's no place like home."

Our Father Helps Us Across the Finish Line

At the 1992 Barcelona Olympics, British track star, Derek Redmond qualified for the 400-meter race with the fastest time in his heat. It looked as if he were headed for gold when suddenly he pulled a hamstring and fell to the ground. Redmond's father ran from the stands, picked him up, and with his arm around his son, he helped him stumble across the finish line.

Our Heavenly Father is committed to this kind of support and assures us He will be there to make sure we finish the race. His strong arms lift us when we fall along the way. He offered His Son, Jesus, as a sacrifice to keep us on track and get us cross the finish line—safely home. God formulated this plan for us before our great grandmothers were born.

Look up. We should be nearing the peak where we can look back with the same excitement the apostle Paul had when he shouted,

> "I have fought the good fight, I have finished the race, I have kept the faith. Now there is in store for me the crown of righteousness, which the Lord, the righteous Judge, will award to me on that day—and not only to me, but also to all who have longed for his appearing" (2 Tim. 4:7–8).

It's God's Timing

An ancient Jewish custom dictated that a young man prepare a place for his new wife. The father watched for the appropriate time to tell his son, "NOW, go get your bride." Even now, Jesus waits for the Father to send Him to get His bride. As a part of His church which is His bride, we're filled with great excitement as we anticipate His coming to carry us across the threshold into the mansion prepared for us in heaven.

A young bride awaits her groom and carefully prepares for her wedding day. We too wait for this joyous occasion. Our desire is to come to Him with clean hands and a pure heart. "I'm baptizing you here in the river, turning your old life in for a kingdom life. His baptism—a holy baptism by the Holy Spirit—will change you from the inside out" (Mark 1:8 MSG). This outward act proclaims to the world that we're ready to die to our old way of life to be raised to experience the new and incredible life with Jesus.

The End May Be Unexpected

The end of the world will come as a bolt of lightning. The galaxies will explode and the elements melt on that final day. But while the world is thrown into panic, we'll watch in awesome wonder, anticipating the glorious new heaven and new earth which will be landscaped with the righteousness of God. All the thorns and thistles of sin will be burned up.

The earth will shudder, the stars explode, and God's thundering voice will reverberate throughout the whole universe. Those who have never bowed in submission to God will drop to their knees at the name of Jesus. Self-sufficiency will vanish. How terrible to face this moment unprepared because they failed to accept Jesus as Lord. "Some of these people have missed the most important thing in life— they don't know God" (1 Tim. 6:21 TLB).

Hearing will be no problem with the last blast of the trumpet. No greater proclamation has ever called the world to stand at attention. It will be the final reveille that wakes the dead. Not only will we hear the sound of the trumpet, but Jesus will call his own, "Come, you who are blessed by my Father; take your inheritance, the kingdom prepared for you since the creation of the world." (Matt. 25:34). How awesome to discover all things have become new. There will be a new heaven, a new earth, a new body, a new home. None of these will ever grow old.

At that time, the curtain will be pulled back to reveal mysteries hidden from the foundation of the world. Revelations about the meaning of life will break forth in the presence of Truth. No doubt there will be a million "ah ha" experiences when we see a reason for every trial, every test we've gone through. "But it is just as the Scriptures say, "What God has planned for people who love him is more than eyes have seen or ears have heard. It has never even entered our minds!" (1 Cor. 2:9 CEV)

Not Good-bye—But So Long

As we stand beside a dying loved one, God can give us words of encouragement: "Go with God, my friend. I will miss you terribly. But one thing I know, it won't be long. Never again will we be separated by distance, but closer than sitting next to each other on the patio or the living room couch with a cup of coffee. It's time for me to turn loose of you, but we're committed never to turn loose of God. I love you now, and I will love you as my forever friend. The best has been saved until last."

I'll take back that metal detector I borrowed in the beginning. The treasure hunt is over. I found my pot of gold at the end of the rainbow of God's promises. Indeed, this has proven to be the golden years.

I found gold while growing old. You can too!

LIFE APPLICATION

1. In the end, what will count as the most meaningful thing in your life?
2. Are you aware that God is willing to do everything you allow Him to—to help you cross the finish line in victory?
3. Are you willing to praise God for planning to accomplish His great purpose in your life?
4. How can the wisdom you learned be passed on to others?
5. Do you see how God is using a refining process in your life?
6. How do you move from coping to hoping?
7. Are you determined to hold on to God until you finish your life here?
8. Are you dealing with habits and hang-ups that stand in the way of your relationship with God and others?
9. How do you plan to meet further challenges that come in your life?
10. Remember that this is the final exam and you will graduate *summa cum laude* when you maintain a good attitude and hold steady with whatever life has handed you.

ABOUT LOUISE

Louise has taught in all levels of education, from elementary school through college. She also taught in the prison system. She managed a Christian Retreat Center for fifteen years and served as the Spiritual Director in a psychiatric hospital. However, she says her greatest accomplishments have been since her mid-seventies when she started going to China to teach in an underground Bible school.

Her writing career began at age seventy-nine. Since then, she has written six books. Her first book received the Selah Award for the "Best Book on Christian Living, 2011."

Louise is a sought-after speaker and was a keynote speaker at the Colorado Christian Writer's Conference in the spring of 2017. There, she was chosen as the "Writer of the Year." A Denver Christian radio station uses humor from her Looney Tidbits on 91 AM, KPOF. She posts "Looney Tidbits" each Friday on social media (www.LooneyTidbits.com).

Her greatest desire is to leave a powerful legacy through her writings and speaking engagements.

BOOKS BY LOUISE

Hidden Treasures for Golden Years—(the book from which this revision is written)
Splashes of Living Water
Marvels and Mysteries
Over the Hill, Onto the Mountaintop
Out of Darkness, Into His Marvelous Light
Make the Rest of Your Days, the Best of Your days—A revision of *Hidden Treasures for Golden Years*

Hidden Treasures for Golden Years, Splashes of Living Water and *Out of Darkness, Into His Marvelous Light* have all been used for a study in home groups.

For more information on Louise's books, visit her website: www.LouiseLLooney.com. Copies may be ordered from Louise or www.Amazon.com.

TO SCHEDULE LOUISE FOR SPEAKING ENGAGMENTS

Contact Louise at louisellooney@gmail.com

TO WATCH HUMOROUS VIDEOS

www.LooneyTidbits.com

Made in the USA
Las Vegas, NV
29 December 2020